AF608181

# PRINCIPLES OF PRIVILEGE

## according to

# THE CODE OF CANON LAW

### A DISSERTATION

*Submitted to the Faculty of Canon Law of the Catholic University of America in partial fulfillment of the requirements for the Degree of Doctor of Canon Law*

*by the*

REV. EDWARD G. ROELKER, S. T. D., J. C. L.,

*of the Archdiocese of Cincinnati.*

WASHINGTON, D. C.

1926

*Nihil Obstat:*

† Thomas J. Shahan,
*Censor Deputatus.*

Washingtonii, D. C. die 6 Maii, 1926.

---

*Imprimatur:*

† Michael J. Curley,
*Archiepiscopus Baltimorensis.*

Baltimorae, die 6 Maii, 1926.

# TABLE OF CONTENTS

## SOURCES.

Acta Apostolicae Sedis, Romae, 1909——.

Acta Sanctae Sedis, Romae, 1865—1908.

Acta et Decreta Concilii Vaticani, Romae, 1872.

Bullarium Romanum, Augustae Taurinorum, 1860.

Codex Iuris Canonici, Romae, 1919.

Codex Theodosianus, Berolini, 1905.

Collectanea S. C. de Propaganda Fide, 2 vol., Romae, 1907.

Corpus Iuris Canonici, 2 vol., Lipsiae, 1922.

Corpus Iuris Civilis, 3 vol., Berlin, 1895.

Decreta S. C. Rituum, 6 vol., Romae, 1901.

Decreta S. C. Tridentini, Taurini, 1913.

Fontes Iuris Canonici, 3 vol., Romae, 1923—1925.

Fonti del Diritto Romano, per cura di Pietro Cogliolo. 2 ed., Torino, 1911.

## BIBLIOGRAPHY.

Aertnys, Joseph, C. SS. R., *Theologia Moralis*, 10 ed., *quam recognitam atque auctam ad Codicem Iuris Canonici accomodavit* C. A. Damen, C. SS. R., Buscoduci, 1919.

Alphonsus, St., de Ligorio, *Theologia Moralis*, Augustae Taurinorum, 1879.

Amort, Eusebius, *Elementa Iuris Canonici Veteris et Moderni*, Ferrariae, 1763.

Antoine, Gabriel, *Theologia Moralis Universa*, Venetiis, 1783.

Arregui, Antonius, S. I., *Summarium Theologiae Moralis*, 5 ed., Bilbao, 1920.

Augustine, Charles, O. S. B., *A Commentary on the New Code of Canon Law*, 4 ed., St. Louis, 1921.

Ayrinhac, H. A., S. S., *General Legislation in the New Code of Canon Law*, New York, 1923.

Bacchinius, Benedictus, O. S. B., *Dissertatio de Ecclesiasticae Hierarchiae Originibus*, Mutinae, 1703.

Ballerini, Antonius, S. I., *Opus Theologicum Morale*, quod edidit Dominicus Palmieri, S. I., Prati, 1889.

Barbosa, Augustinus, *Tractatus Varii*, Lugduni, 1660.

Bargilliat, M., *Praelectiones Iuris Canonici*, Parisiis, 1918.

Bartholinus, Joannes Baptista, *De Subreptione Rescriptorum*, Venetiis, 1601.

Bellarminus, Robertus Cardinalis, S. I., *Opera Omnia*, *vol. I*, Neapoli, 1872.

Benedictus XIV, (Prosper Lambertini), *De Synodo Diocesana*, Romae, 1806.

Benedictus XIV, *Consultationes Canonicae et Morales*, *Opera Omnia*, *vol. XII, XIII*, Romae, 1884.

Blat, Albertus, O. P., *Commentarium in Textum Iuris Canonici*, Romae, 1921.

Bonacina, Martinus, *Opera Omnia de Theologia Morali*, Lugduni, 1634.

Bonfante, Pietro, *Storia del Diritto Romano*, Milano, 1909.

Bouix, D., *De Principiis Iuris Canonici*, Parisiis, 1882.

Bouix, D., *De Iure Regularium*, Parisiis, 1882.

Bouquillon, Thomas, *Theologia Moralis Fundamentalis*, Brugis, 1890.

Brandys, Maximilian, O. F. M., *Kirchliches Rechtsbuch*, Paderborn, 1920.

Brys, J., *De Dispensatione in Iure Canonico*, Brugis, 1925.

Bucceroni, Ianuarius, S. I., *Casus Conscientiae*, 6 ed., Romae, 1913.

Calvinus, (Johannes Kahl) *Magnum Lexicon Iuridicum*, Coloniae Allobrogum, 1759.

Cardenas, Ioannes, S. I., *Crisis Theologica*, Venetiis, 1700.

Cartagena, Bartholomaeus, *Expositio Titulorum Iuris Canonici*, Lugduni, 1624.

Chelodi, Ioannes, *Ius de Personis*, Tridenti, 1922.

Cicognani, Hamletus, *Commentarium ad Librum I Codicis*, Romae, 1925.

Cocchi, Guidus, C. M., *Commentarium in Codicem Iuris Canonici*, Taurinorum Augustae, 1921.

Craisson, D., *Manuale totius Iuris Canonici*, 4 ed., Pictavii, 1875.

D'Annibale, Iosephus Cardinalis, *Summula Theologiae Moralis*, Romae, 1908.

DeAngelis, Philippus, *Praelectiones Iuris Canonici*, Romae, 1877.

DeCamillis, P., *Institutiones Iuris Canonici*, Parisiis, 1868.

DeMeester, A., *Compendium Iuris Canonici et Iuris Canonico-Civilis*, Brugis, 1921.

Demeuron, J. Louis, *L'Eglise*, Paris, 1914.

Devoti, Ioannes, *Institutionum Canonicarum libri IV*, Romae, 1825.

Fagnanus, Prosper, *Commentarium in Libros Decretalium,* Venetiis, 1729.

Fanfani, Ludovicus, O. P., *De Iure Religiosorum,* Taurini Romae, 1925.

Ferreres, Ioannes, S. I., *Institutiones Canonicae,* Barcinone, 1920.

Ferraris, Lucius, *Prompta Bibliotheca Canonica,* Parisiis, 1865.

Ferrini, Contardo, *Manuale di Pandette,* Milano, 1917.

Fuhrich, Maximilianus, S. I., *De Religiosis,* Oeniponte, 1919.

Genicot, Eduardus, S. I., *Institutiones Theologiae Moralis,* 9 et 10 ed., Bruxellis, 1921-22.

Glaire, J. B., *Dictionnaire,* Paris, 1868.

Grandclaude, E., *Ius Canonicum,* Parisiis, 1883.

Harris, Seymour F., *Elements of Roman Law,* London, 1875.

Herincx, Gulielmus, *Summa Theologica Scholastica et Moralis,* Antwerpiae, 1680.

Hostiensis, Henrici Cardinalis, *Summa Aurea,* Venetiis, 1570.

Humphrey, William, S. J., *Conscience and Law,* London, 1896.

Lega, Michael, *Praelectiones de Iudiciis Ecclesiasticis,* 2 ed., Romae, 1905.

Leitner, Martin, *Handbuch des Katholischen Kirchenrechts,* 2 ed., Regensburg, 1922.

Manzi, J. D., *Epitome Iuris Canonici,* Mechliniae, 1824.

Maroto, Philippus, *Institutiones Iuris Canonici,* 3 ed., Romae, 1921.

Martin, Michael, S. J., *The Roman Curia,* London, 1913.

Makee, Ch., *Institutiones Iuris Ecclesiastici,* Parisiis, 1897.

Massimi, Maximus, *Introductio in Gai et Justiniani Institutiones,* Romae, 1910.

Massimi, Maximus, *Interpretatio Gai et Justiniani Institutionum,* Cryptaeferratae, 1917.

Menghini, Ioannes Baptista, *Elementa Iuris Liturgici*, Romae, 1906.

Mothon, Joseph, O. P., *Institutions Canoniques*, Paris, 1922.

Motry, Hubert L., *Diocesan Faculties*, Washington, 1922.

Nannetti, Emedio, *Brevi Nozioni di Diritto Publico Ecclesiastico*, Bologna, 1840.

Noldin, H., S. I., *De Principiis Theologiae Moralis*, 13 ed., Oeniponte, 1921.

Noval, Iosephus, O. P., *Commentarium Codicis Iuris Canonici lib. IV, Pars I, De Iudiciis*, Augustae Taurinorum, 1920.

Palao, Ferdinandus, S. I., *Opus Morale, vol. I*, Lugduni, 1682.

Papi, Hector, S. J., *Religious in Church Law*, New York, 1924.

Pesch, Christianus, S. L., *Praelectiones Dogmaticae*, Friburgi Briscoviae, 1924.

Pirhing, Ernicus, S. I., *Ius Canonicum*, Dillingae, 1674.

Prummer, Dominicus, O. P., *Manuale Iuris Canonici*, 2 ed., Friburgi Briscoviae, 1920.

Prummer, Dominicus, O. P., *Manuale Theologiae Moralis*, Friburgi Briscoviae, 1923.

Putzer, Ioseph, C. SS. R., *Commentarium in Facultates Apostolicas*, Neo Eboraci, 1893.

Raus, I. B., C. SS. R., *Institutiones Canonicae*, Lugduni-Parisiis, 1923.

Reiffenstuel, Anacletus, *Ius Canonicum Universum*, Antwerpiae, 1743.

Sanchez, Thomas, *De Sancto Matrimonii Sacramento*, Antwerpiae, 1626.

Sanguineti, Sebastianus, *Institutiones Iuris Ecclesiastici Privati*, Romae, 1884.

Santi, Franciscus, *Praelectiones Iuris Canonici*, Ratisbonae, 1886.

Schaefer, Timotheus, O. M. Cap., *Das Ordensrecht*, Munster, 1923.

Schmalzgrueber, Franciscus, S. I., *Ius Ecclesiasticum*, Romae, 1845.

Sebastianelli, Gulielmus, *Praelectiones Iuris Canonici, De Personis*, Romae, 1905.

Sebastianelli, Gulielmus, *Praelectiones Iuris Canonici, De Iudiciis Ecclesiasticis*, Romae, 1906.

Sherer, Rudolf von, *Handbuch des Kirchenrechts*, Graz, 1886.

Slater, Thomas, S. J., *A Manual of Moral Theology*, New York, 1908.

Smith, William, *A Dictionary of Greek and Roman Antiquities*, London, 1875.

Smith, S. B., *Elements of Ecclesiastical Law*, New York, 1877.

Soglia, Ioannes Cardinalis, *Institutiones Iuris Publici et Privati Ecclesiastici*, 10 ed., Boscoduci, sine anno.

Sohm, Rudolph, *Institutes of Roman Law*, Oxford, 1892.

Solieri, Franciscus, *Institutiones Iuris Ecclesiastici*, Romae, 1921.

Suarez, Franciscus, S. I., *Opera Omnia, vol. V, VI.*, Parisiis, 1856.

Tamburini, Thomas, S. I., *Opera Omnia, vol. II*, Venetiis, 1702.

Trudel, P. SS., *A Dictionary of Canon Law*, St. Louis, 1920.

Tuschus, Dominicus Cardinalis, *Conclusiones Practicae Iuris*, Lugduni, 1634.

Vecchiotti, Septimius, *Institutiones Canonicae*, Taurini, 1867.

Vermeersch, A., S. I., Creusen, I., S. I., *Epitome Iuris Canonici*, Mechliniae-Romae, 1921.

Wernz, Franciscus, S. I., *Ius Decretalium, tom. I*, Prati, 1913.

Wernz, Franciscus, S. I., *Ius Canonicum, tom. II, De Personis, opera* Petri Vidal, S. I., Romae, 1923.

Winslow, Francis J., *Vicars and Prefects Apostolic*, New York, 1924.

Woywod, Stanislaus, O. F. M., *A Practical Commentary on the Code of Canon Law*, New York, 1925.
Zallinger, Iacobus, *Institutiones Iuris Ecclesiastici*, Romae, 1832.
Zallinger, Iacobus, *Institutionum Iuris Naturalis et Ecclesiastici Publici libri V*, Romae, 1823.
Zoesius, Henricus Iacobus, *Commentarium in Ius Canonicum Universum*, Venetiis, 1757.

## FOREWORD.

The Code of Canon Law groups the principles regulating privileges in the canons comprising the fifth title of the first book. All privileges are to be governed according to these principles, no matter whether the privilege be granted by the law itself, or be conceded outside of the field of law.

The purpose of this dissertation will be to examine the seventeen canons under the title *De Privilegiis.*

In accordance with the general theme of the entire first book of the Code, consideration will be restricted to principles which govern privileges. Hence, no single privilege will be subjected either to historical scrutiny, or to a review of its canonical development. Beyond their obvious utility in exemplifying principles, the privileges of the Code will not be discussed.

In general, the order of the Code will be followed. One exception to this order will be made in discussing the canon on "faculties." Since these faculties are entirely *praeter ius,* it was deemed advisable to place the chapter on "faculties" after the chapters which consider all classes of privileges.

# CHAPTER I

## FUNDAMENTAL IDEAS CONCERNING PRIVILEGES IN ECCLESIASTICAL LAW.

In a treatise on privileges it is necessary to mention and explain all the various concepts which possess either a direct, or an indirect relation to the subject of privileges. The object of this first chapter will be to set down the fundamental ideas of "privilege", some of which will recur again and again thru the body of this dissertation.

### 1. *Etymology and early use of the word "privilege".*

The English word "privilege" is a translation of the Latin noun *privilegium.* The letter is derived from the adjective *privus,* and the noun *lex.*[1] *Privus* means "single," or "individual": thus *privus homo* means an individual man.[2]

When considering the use of the word "privilege," a distinction must be made between ante-Augustan writers, and post-Augustan writers. Near the beginning of the Christian era the usual concept of "privilege" changed completely. It still held the idea of something individual, but the object of a privilege was altered entirely.

In the time of Cicero, the word "privilege" had

---

1 Harper's *Latin Dictionary,* (New York, 1888), v. privilegium; Antoine, *Theologia Moralis Universa,* (Venetiis, 1783), tom. II, p. 85, ad calcem 1 records a double etymology of the word *privilegium,* (1) *privans lege-eximens a lege,* (2) *lex privata-speciale aliquid concedens;* cf. Cartegena, *Expositio Titulorum Iuris Canonici,* (Lugduni, 1624), lib. V, tit. XXXIII, p. 459.

2 *Privos privasque antiqui dicebant pro singulis: ob quam causam et privata dicuntur quae uniuscuiusque sint, hinc et privilegium et privatus,* Cogliolo, *Manuale delle Fonti del Diritto* Romano, (Torino, 1911), 2 ed., *De verborum significatione,* n. VIII.

predominantly an odious meaning. It meant an ordinance made against a single person. Such an ordinance was not according to the customs of the Romans. Cicero writes: *in privatos homines leges ferri noluerunt: id est enim privilegium.*[3] With the Romans a law was an ordinance of general interest. Such a departure, then, as an individual ordinance was abhorrent to Cicero. He adds pointedly: *quo quid est iniustius?* However such a procedure was not unknown. Cicero himself refers to a privilege in his fourth Paradox,[4] and his own fortunes were visited with a similar law. In defense of his own property, Cicero eloquently remarks: *Vetant leges sacratae, vetant XII tabulae leges*[5] *privatis hominibus inrogari: id est enim privilegium. Nemo unquam tulit; nihil est crudelius, nihil perniciosius, nihil quod minus haec civitas ferre possit.*[6]

During the time of Augustus, the word "privilege" was used in the sense of a favor, or a prerogative. It was no longer used in an odious sense. Seneca writes of privileges which were granted to parents.[7] He speaks of favors and calls them *beneficia.* This word expressed good will: *in beneficiis iucundissima sit tribuentis voluntas.*[8]

Roman Law took up this new meaning of "privi-

---

3 *De Legibus,* lib. III, c. 19; lib. III, c. 4, M. Tulii Ciceronis, recognovit C.F.W. Mueller, Scripta quae manserunt omnia, P. IV, v. II, (Lipsiae, 1905).

4 *Familiarissimus tuus de te privilegium tulit. Paradoxa IV, o.c.,* p. IV, v. III, (Lipsiae, 1898).

5 *Privicloes leges ne irroganto;* Tab. IX, n. 8, Cogliolo, *o.c.*

6 *Pro domo sua,* n. 17; M. Tulii Orationes, recognovit Gulielmus Peterson, (Oxonii, sine anno).

7 *Quaedam privilegia parentibus datae sunt; De Beneficiis,* lib. III, c. XI, (Lipsiae, 1900) L. Annaei Senecae opera quae supersunt, v. I, fasc. II, edidit Carolus Hosius.

8 *De Beneficiis, o.c.,* lib. II, c. I.

lege,"[9] and altho concessions and favors were not always spoken of as privileges, yet one who enjoyed such a right was known as *privilegiarius.*[10]

2. *Ius singulare in Roman Law.*

In Roman Law there existed an institution known as *ius singulare.* This was a law which had for its purpose some special utility beyond the common utility of all law.[11] Thus one category of creditors was preferred to another,[12] donations between husband and wife were invalid,[13] etc. The jurist Paulus wrote: *Ius singulare est quod contra tenorem rationis propter aliquam utilitatem auctoritate constituentium introductum est.*[14] But it would be erroneous to say that utility was the sole standard of *ius singulare,* and it is better to say with Ferrini[15] that in the case of *ius singulare* the aspect of utility was more in evidence than usual.

A privilege bears some similarity to the Roman *ius singulare.*[16] Both were given in view of individual persons, or groups, but while a privilege frequently remained a simple concession, *ius singulare* often represented an advance in legislation and thus became incorporated in succeeding general codifications of law.[17] The embodiment of many *iura singularia* gave a development

---

9 Thus in the Theodosian Code: *Etiam istud adjungimus, ut domos etiam clementiae nostrae, quas vetusta et innumera ab huius oneris curatione privilegia vindicabant, par conditio et sollicitudo constringat, ita tamen, ut in ceteris quae vel inlustribus vel patrimonio nostro praecedentibus edictis beneficia fuerant adtributa, intemerata permaneant:* XV, 3, 4. (Berolini, 1905), cf. also XIV, 2, 1.

10 *Ulpian,* D. 14, 5, 3; cf. Calvinus, *Magnum Lexicon Iuridicum,* (Coloniae Allobrogum, 1759), verb. privilegiarius.

11 Ferrini, *Manuale di Pandette,* (Milano, 1917), n. 9.

12 D. 42, 3, 1.

13 D. 24, 1, 1.

14 D. 1, 3, 16.

15 Ferrini, *o.c.,* l.c.

16 D'Annibale, *Summula Theologiae Moralis,* (Romae, 1908), v. I, n. 227, ad calcem 1.

17 Ferrini, *o.c.,* n. 10.

to law which really represented mighty strides in jurisprudence.

### 3. *Law.*

Since so many canonists have used the word "law" in their definition of a privilege, a few thoughts must be set down relative to what a law really is. Saint Thomas[18] defined a law as *ordinatio rationis ad bonum commune ab eo qui communitatis curam habet promulgata.* Suarez[19] gave a somewhat similar definition: *commune praeceptum iustum ac stabile sufficienter promulgata.*

The elements of a law are (a) general obligation, (b) proper matter, (c) competent authority, and (d) promulgation.[20] The first element necessarily excludes every ordinance which does not refer to all the subjects in a community, or society. The second characteristic demands a just regulation, and apt material. The third element restricts the issuance of a law to those who actually enjoy legislative power, The power may be in temporal matters or in spirtiual. The last note of a law requires that the subject be made cognizant of the law. This does not mean that everyone must individually be acquainted with the details of the law. In many cases this would be impossible; it suffices to have the law made public.

An ecclesiastical law must fulfill the same requirements as any other law. It could then be defined thus: *ordinatio rationis ad bonum commune ab eo qui communitatis ecclesiasticae curam habet promulgata.*[21] Ecclesiastical law, however, differs in one important respect from civil law: its history does not begin with custom. The law of the Church existed in earliest times as can

18 1.2. qu. 90. a. 4.
19 Suarez, *Opera Omnia,* (Parisiis, 1856), v. V, lib. I, c, 12, n. 1.
20 Herincx, *Summa Theologica Scholastica et Moralis,* (Antwerpiae, 1680), tr. III, disp. I, q. I, n. 1-5.
21 Wernz, *Ius Decretalium,* (Prati, 1913), tom. I, n. 89.

be seen from the ordinances laid down by the Apostles.[22] Subsequent to these laws customs arose. Ancient civil law does not enjoy this priority. Roman Law found much of its source in customs, as did also Greek and barbarian law.[23]

### 4. *The Concept of Privilege in Ecclesiastical Law.*

As has been observed, the etymology of the word "privilege" demands that a privilege be a provision made in regard to a single person. A moral person, or body with proper approbation can also be considered juridically as a single person. Beyond this the idea of individuality cannot be extended.[24] A provision in regard to either of these two divisions can be understood as a privilege.

Now let the favorable idea of a privilege be considered. Ecclesiastical law was founded at a time when the original, unfavorable meaning of the word "privilege" had been discarded, and the new, benevolent idea was in vogue.[25] This meaning has ever since remained to the total exclusion of the ante-Augustan signification.[26] Hence a privilege would be a favorable provision in respect of a physical, or moral person.

Then, were a comparison instituted between a privilege and the elements of a law, it will be seen that the purpose of a privilege is directly opposed to the purpose

---

22 Wernz, *o.c.*, *l.c.*

23 Massini, *Interpretatio Gai et Iustiniani Institutionum*, (Cryptaeferratae, 1907), p. 12.

24 Non-collegiate moral persons can also be the subject of privilege.

25 Cicognani, *Commentarium ad Librum I Codicis*, (Romae, 1925), p. 273.

26 Privilege in civil law was also called ius singulare, beneficium, rescriptum, diploma Principale, constitutio personalis, favor, auxilium, gratia; cf. Calvinus, *o.c.*, verb. privilegium; in ecclesiastical law, privilege was also called rescriptum, diploma, indultum, principale, favor, gratia, immunitas; cf. Reiffenstuel, *Ius Canonicum Universum*, (Antwerpiae, 1743), lib. V, tit. XXXIII, n. 6: Glaire, *Dictionnaire Universel des Sciences Ecclesiastiques*, (Paris, 1868), adds loi favorable, prerogative, avantage, droit particulier, verb. privilege.

of a law. In no direct way can a privilege as such be said to be *ad bonum commune.* Yet this is essential in a law. Lacking this element a privilege of itself cannot be a law. Add to this the idea of free acceptance, and use of a privilege on the part of the grantee. Free acceptance, however, is not absolutely essential to the concept of a strict privilege because a privilege can actually be granted without the consent of the grantee.[27]

The two concepts of law and privilege thus diverge more and more. In fact only one important point seems to be common to both law and privilege, and this of necessity. This point is the source whence come both privilege and law. The legislator is the author of law, explicit in legislation, tacit in custom, as he is also of privilege. After this common element is disposed of, perhaps nothing more remains under which both concepts might be grouped.

Still the idea of stability, or duration might be urged as a common element. Altho this could be admitted, the admission would not identify privilege and law in a generic way. Yet it is this stability which gives some appearance of a law to a privilege.[28]

The privileges enumerated in the Code are not all strict privileges. None of these privileges can be rejected, but must be accepted together with the dignity, or state to honor which these privileges are conceded. Thus a Cardinal, or Bishop cannot reject his privileges once his dignity has been conferred upon him. In fact Prelates implicitly accept their privileges when they accept their dignity. Similarly, clerics cannot reject their clerical privileges, nor can Regulars, considered as individuals, or as a community reject their privilege of exemption. This necessity of accepting the privileges con-

---

27 Maroto, *Institutiones Iuris Canonici,* (Romae, 1921) 3 ed., v. I, n. 291.
28 Cocchi, *Commentarium in Codicem Iuris Canonici,* (Taurinorum Augustae, 1921), v. I, 113-4.

tained in the Code would not itself destroy the idea of a strict privilege, because these privileges are granted in view of the exalted position, or higher state in life obtained or chosen by the grantee. These privileges, therefore, are not conceded solely because of the grantee.

Liberty in using, or not using the privileges granted by the Code will indicate whether or not such privileges are strict privileges. While a Cardinal, or Bishop cannot reject his privileges, yet he can neglect their use. Neither Prelate is obliged to bless rosaries whenever an occasion presents itself. Neither Prelate is obliged to celebrate mass on a portable altar. The use of these privileges depends upon the wishes of the grantee. Such privileges can be compared favorably with concessions found outside of the law. One practical difference can be noted. Legislators and judges are presumed to be acquainted with the grants made in law, but are presumed to be unacquainted with the grants outside of the field of law. Therefore the latter grants would have to be proved in order to be sustained, while presumption favors the grantee who receives his privilege from the law itself.[29]

On the other hand, the privileges of clerics must be used whenever an occasion warrants. A cleric cannot forego *privilegium canonis* and submit to injury.[30] In the same way ecclesiastical court cannot be neglected and civil court used in trials.[31] Similarly, an exempt religious cannot place himself under the jurisdiction of the Ordinary of the diocese where he may be residing. This same

---

29 Cf. D'Annibale, *o.c.,* v. I, n. 277 ad calcem (1); This author limits strict privileges to grants made outside of law. His definition of privilege is: *beneficium principis extra corpus iuris alicui concessum.* After the Code, Maroto, v. I, n. 291, and Cocchi, v. I, n. 113-114 use the same distinction so that the Code would contain absolutely no privileges in the strict sense of the word.

30 C. 15, X, *de sententia excommunicationis,* V, 39.

31 Cf. can. 120, 1,2, for necessary permission to act in civil court: Wernz-Vidal, *De Personis,* (Romae, 1923), n. 77.

prohibition attaches to the entire exempt religious institute. Hence, since clerical privileges, and the privilege of exemption can neither be rejected nor neglected, the beneficiaries of these privileges have practically no control over their privileges. Consequently such privileges are called *privilegia late sumpta.* However it must be borne in mind that *privilegium late sumptum* is not thereby an improper privilege, or that the word "privilege" is employed merely in an accommodated sense. A real concession is made, and the word "privilege" is properly employed, as the Code itself indicates.[32] But since little control, if any, of these privileges is left to the grantee, they can only be called *late sumpta.*

In regard to privileges granted outside of the Code, the same characteristic, *i. e.,* freedom in using a privilege, will determine whether or not a privilege is *stricto,* or *lato sensu.* Privileges in particular law will be judged according to this norm. Concessions outside of both common and particular law will usually be strict privileges.

A paragraph concerning the negative aspect of a privilege will complete this discussion. Positive law does not state that special rights conceded by means of privileges are not to be used by non-privileged persons. Altho such a statement would clearly set off the distinct characteristic of a privilege (*favor specialis*), yet it is scarcely necessary to state categorically that special rights are not to be used unless specifically granted. The law is the general standard of rights as well as of obligations. Any right outside of law must, in some way, be the result of special concession.

Completing the distinction between privileges strictly so called and privileges widely so called, it is necessary to state that unless the context demand otherwise, a strict privilege is meant in this dissertation.

32 E.g., Can. 123, 618.

### 5. *Privilege in the Decree of Gratian, and in the Decretals of Gregory IX.*

Gratian taught: *Privilegia sunt leges privatorum, quasi privatae leges. Nam privilegium inde dictum est, quod in privato feratur.*[33] Altho Gratian understands privileges as laws, yet he could scarcely have meant a law in the strict sense of the word. In the very next distinction[34] Gratian gives the qualifications of a law. *Erit autem lex honesta, iusta, possibilis, secundum naturam, secundum consuetudinem patriae, loco temporique conveniens, necessaria, utilis, manifesta quoque, ne aliquid per obscuritatem inconveniens contineat,* NULLO PRIVATO COMMODO, SED PRO COMMUNI UTILITATE CIVIUM CONSCRIPTA. In both citations Gratian's authority is Isidore.[35]

Glossa[36] interprets the word *leges* to mean strict laws, but this contention is based on the use of this word as contained in a Decretal of Pope Innocent III.[37]

After describing the contentions of two abbeys relative to the appointment of an Abbot, Innocent III says that a privilege is a private law.[38] It is scarcely likely that Pope Innocent meant to define a privilege as a real law, because the case he has in mind only concerns the monks of the two abbeys in question, and in no wise fulfills all the requirements of a law, common good, promulgation, etc. Arguing from the concession granted by Pope Paschal, confirmed by Pope Callixtus II, Innocent III decides that the privilege is legitimate and must be hon-

---

33 C. 3, D. III.

34 C. 2, D. IV.

35 For privilege: *Etym.* lib. V, c. 18, n. 1, MPL. v. 82, col. 202; for law: *Etym.* lib. II, c. 10, n. 6, MPL v. 82, col. 131.

36 Glossa is helpful in giving the use of the word *privati.* Privati sunt: (a) *non constituti in aliqua dignitate,* (b) *excepti a iure communi sive sit collegium, sive sit aliqua specialis persona.*

37 C. 25, X, *de verborum significatione,* V, 40.

38 *Quum privilegium sit lex privata;* c. 25, X, *de verborum significatione,* V, 40.

ored. Certainly the monks of Saint Silvan's abbey, who acted in opposition to the privilege given to the other monastery, were obliged to live up to the terms of the privilege. But this obligation arises fundamentally from natural law: no one is allowed to infringe the rights of another. It is true that this can be called an obligation resulting from a privilege, but it is not enough to make a strict law of a privilege.

In the case at hand the monks of Saint Bertin, who enjoyed the privilege of having one of their number elected Abbot of Saint Silvan's abbey, were not obliged to use their privilege. But in fact it is their continued and tenacious use of their privilege (thru the election of seven Abbots) which makes their case so strong with Innocent III. The monks went so far as to require a certain Guarinus, a monk of Saint Silvan's, to make his profession in the abbey of Saint Bertin, and there remain for a time before the Abbot would consent to his election as the head of the abbey of Saint Silvan.[39]

### 6. *Various definitions of Privilege.*

An argument from strict juridical principles does not destroy the clause *quum privilegium sit lex privata.*[40] Suarez[41] for one held a privilege to be a strict law. Since Suarez is one of the principal adherents of this opinion, it would be well to outline his doctrine on the matter rather fully. Suarez[42] says that every just law which does not impose a special and odious obligation is in a certain sense a privilege. One reason is because of its directive nature.[43] Suarez then shows the double accepta-

[39] In a recent work Brys, *De Dispensatione in Iure Canonico,* (Brugis, 1925), claims that commentators on the Decretals did not draw a strict line of demarcation between privileges and dispensations. Some indeed identified the two concepts. p. 101, 168-9.

[40] C. 25, X, *de verborum significatione,* V, 40.

[41] Suarez, *o.c.,* lib. VIII, c. 1, n. 2.

[42] Suarez, *o.c.,* lib. VIII, pr.

[43] *Illuminat, dirigit, et in officio continet,* l.c.

tion of the word *privilegium*:[44] the word means either the favor conceded, or the document in which the favor is contained. Next Suarez says that not every privilege is a law, because some favors are not perpetual.[45] Stability is Suarez's standard. If a favor is not permanent, but is given for a certain time, it is not a law. Constructing his definition philosophically, Suarez uses the word *lex* as the genus, and the word *privata* taken from Innocent III,[46] as the species. The favorable aspect is taken from the object of the privilege. Completed, the definition reads: *lex privata aliquid speciale concedens*.[47]

Suarez will not admit that the word *privata* destroys the idea of a strict law, but, instead, makes the word a characteristic by which a privilege is distinguished from other laws.[48]

But Suarez is forced somewhat to recede from his position when he discusses the necessity of promulgation.[49] Then he maintains that many concessions do not receive promulgation. Suarez is obliged to concede that natural law at least supplies the fundamental reason for the non-interference with a privilege. Suarez takes refuge in the fact that the privileged person must exhibit a document to prove his concession, should it be challenged. Thus this simple form of proof supplies the notice which a community must have to respect a privilege.

Suarez is incorrect in his classification of a privilege. Stripped of some of the essential elements of a real law, namely, direct obligation, common observance, and promulgation, the only notes which remain common to privilege and law are source and stability. Both law

44 Suarez, *o.c.*, lib. VIII, c. 1, n. 1.
45 Suarez, *o.c.*, *l.c.*
46 C. 25, X, *de verborum significatione*, V, 40.
47 Suarez, *o.c.*, lib. VIII, c. 1, n. 3.
48 Suarez, *o.c.*, *l.c.*
49 Suarez, *o.c.*, lib. VIII, c. 24, n. 7.

and privilege come from the same legislator, and both can have equal permanence. But this is not sufficient to put the two canonical institutes in the same category.

Cardinal Hostiensis[50] was another canonist who considered a privilege to be a law. He draws his support from Gratian and Innocent III. Consequently, it would be superfluous to repeat the remarks on the interpretation of the sources. The same reasons for maintaining that neither Gratian, nor Innocent III had used the phrase *lex privata* in the strict sense also militate against the propriety of Hostiensis' definition of privilege.

Herincx[51] gives a definition for privilege which is not better the Suarez's definition. He writes: *Privilegium est constitutio principis specialem favorem concedens.* A privilege gives the right either to perform some action, or to omit it.

An analysis of the elements of Herincx's definition of privilege will reveal how unacceptable it is. *Constitutio* is usually a document which founds a general law.[52] Accepted in this sense, Herincx's definition falls into Suarez's error, and it must be rejected, for a privilege is not a law since the latter must be issued for general observance. Besides, *constitutio* allows only for a privilege which is found in writing. This would not be sufficiently extensive as a privilege can also be obtained by custom and prescription.[53] The word *principis* is misleading, for it does not seem to cover all competent Superiors. A better expression would have been *auctoritatis competentis.* In using the latter expression every Superior is held within his own province, and the legitimate power of Superiors inferior to the Roman Pontiff is recognized.

50 Hostiensis, *Summa Aurea,* (Venetiis, 1570), lib. V, in tit. *de privilegiis et excessibus privilegiatorum,* n. 1.

51 Herincx, *o.c.,* tr. 3, disp. 4, q. 3, n. 53.

52 Maroto, *o.c.,* v. I, n. 238.

53 Can. 63, § 1.

Reiffenstuel's definition of privilege is: *Lex privata contra, vel praeter ius aliquid concedens.*[54] Reiffenstuel admits there is no obligation in respect of the privileged person, but merely in regard to the community which must not interfere with the privilege. In explaining why there is no obligation in respect of the grantee, Reiffenstuel says *nemo beneficio sibi concesso uti cogitur.* This statement is enough to weaken Reiffenstuel's definition of privilege. If the principal beneficiary is under no obligation to use his privilege, the concession is anything but a strict law, for a law imposes a direct obligation on those for whom it is enacted. *Concessio,* or *donatio* would have been a better word in Reiffenstuel's definition, and not the word *lex,* even if the last-named word is qualified by the adjective *privata.*

Some modern authors, such as Wernz,[55] and Blat[56] retain Suarez's definition of privilege. Their explanation is practically the same, and it is founded similarly on the text of Innocent III.[57] A phrase approaching *lex privata* is used by Vermeersch.[58] He defines a privilege thus: *ius singulare quibusdam concessum.* This definition is not entirely acceptable. Granted that the noun *ius* is used properly to mean a right, or faculty, nevertheless it stresses the object of a privilege rather than its formal element. An earlier and somewhat different definition of privilege was given by Grandclaude.[59] *Privilegium est ius singulare contra vel praeter tenorem iuris communis, ob aliquam utilitatem a principe concessum.* In his explanation of his definition, Grandclaude makes

---

54 Reiffenstuel, *o.c.,* lib. V, tit. XXXIII, n. 3.

55 Wernz, *o.c.,* v. I, n. 158.

56 Blat, *Commentarium in Textum Codicis Iuris Canonici,* (Romae, 1921) v. I, n. 129.

57 C. 25, X, *de verborum significatione,* V, 40.

58 Vermeersch-Creusen, *Epitome Iuris Canonici,* (Mechliniae-Romae, 1921), v. I, n. 128.

59 Grandclaude, *Ius Canonicum,* (Parisiis, 1883), lib. V, tit. XXXIII, n. 1.

*ius* almost synonymous with *lex.* For this reason his definition is unacceptable.

Passing from an account of authors who more or less stressed the idea of law in their definitions of privilege, there remain to be examined several definitions which indeed use the word *lex,* but explain it so that only an analogical resemblance exists between privilege and law.

The Jesuit canonist, Schmalzgrueber, preserved the form of Suarez's definition of privilege, but explained it in a far different fashion.[60] A privilege is a private law, but only analogically, and improperly so called. With this explanation the phrase private law can remain in a definition of privilege since one of the effects of a privilege is non-interference with the use of a privilege. Altho this effect primarily arises from the natural law, as Herincx admits,[61] yet it is often embodied in the concession itself so that no excuse may be left to the transgressor. Human ingenuity can devise various methods of interfering with, or hampering the pacific use of a privilege. The result would be that the benevolent will of the legislator would be thwarted. That such interference occurred in the past, the following Decretal of Honorius III will show.

The monks of Cluny could not be excommunicated by the Ordinaries of the dioceses in which the Cluniac monasteries were situated. Some of the officials, however, indirectly violated the rights of the monks in obliging them to suffer the effects of excommunication. Thus in preserving the letter of the monks' privilege, for they did not formally pass sentence of excommunication, the officials nevertheless infringed on the rights of the monks. Hearing of this dissimulation, the Pope ordered the offi-

---

60 Schmalzgrueber, *Ius Ecclesiasticum,* (Romae, 1845), lib. V, tit. XXXIII, n. 2-3.

61 Herincx, *o.c.,* tr. 3, disp. 4, q. 4, n. 53.

cials to cease their activities, and obey both the letter and the spirit of the monks' privilege.[62]

While the definition of Schmalzgrueber might reasonably be accepted yet for purposes of clarity, it is not perfect. A definition should be clear and concise, leaving no room for misunderstanding. Consequently, whenever possible error may arise from the wording of a definition, it should be recast, and presented in another form.

One of the latest canonists to write on privileges still retains the expression *lex privata*. But like Schmalzgrueber, Cicognani[63] explains his definition in such a way that the idea of a strict law is destroyed, leaving merely an analogical and improper meaning.

Woywod[64] also uses the expression "private law," but deprecates the use of this expression because it cannot be upheld at least in the provisions granted to individual persons.

Sanguineti gives a definition of privilege which seems to be acceptable. *Privilegium est concessio permanens alicuius iuris specialis a legitimo Superiore facta.*[65] In this definition the nature of privilege is correctly described as a concession. Thus the beneficiary is not obliged to accept the right granted for a concession usually implies voluntary acceptance of the provision. This note of free acceptance is even acknowledged by those who claim that a privilege is a strict law.[66]

Custom and prescription are also sources of privilege.[67] Hence it is necessary to understand Sanguineti's *concessio* as including legal concession.

---

62 C. 20, X, *de privilegiis et excessibus privilegiatorum*, V, 33; cf. also c. 7-11, C. XXV, q. 2.

63 Cicognani, *o.c.*, p. 273.

64 Woywod, *A practical Commentary on the Code of Canon Law*, (New York, 1925), v. I, n. 46.

65 Sanguineti, *Institutiones Iuris Ecclesiastici Privati*, (Romae, 1884), n. 137.

66 Reiffenstuel, *o.c.*, lib. V, tit. XXXIII, n. 3.

67 Can. 63, § 1.

The idea of permanence as contained in a privilege is not essential to the nature of a privilege, and for this reason it could be omitted from the definition of privilege.

The phrase *alicuius iuris specialis* is well used for a privilege grants a right which is otherwise unattainable, either in itself or in its permanence. This idea of speciality is so necessary to a privilege that without it a privilege would be unintelligible. The common law gives certain rights. If a privilege did no more than this it would be practically useless.

The necessary competence of Superiors is well expressed in Sanguineti's definition of privilege. This idea will be developed in the next chapter.

Cocchi[68] defines privilege in the same way as Sanguineti. Before the Code, Makee[69] used practically the same definition.

In this dissertation Sanguineti's definition of privilege will be adopted. However, the word *permanens* will be omitted since it does directly touch the essence of a privilege. With this omission the definition of privilege reads: *Privilegium est concessio alicuius iuris specialis a legitimo Superiore facta.*

7. *A proportionate cause relative to a privilege.*

(*a*) *For the validity of a privilege.* The will of the legislator is the sole force upon which obedience to the law rests. Hence the obligation to obey the law can change in whatever way the legislator alters his will. A proportionate cause is not necessary in order that a legislator may change his will, and consequently a proportionate cause is not necessary for the concession of a privilege. Schmalzgrueber[70] classes a privilege as a kind of

68 Cocchi, *o.c.*, v. I, n. 114.
69 Makee, *Institutiones Iuris Ecclesiastici*, (Parisiis, 1897).
70 Schmalzgrueber, *o.c.*, lib. V, tit. XXXIII, n. 17.

donation. But a donation can be made without cause, and hence a privilege. Reiffenstuel[71] says a legislator can remove a law *ex toto*, and in the same way *ex parte*, as he does in a privilege. Pirhing[72] adds no more but uses the argument from the will of the legislator.

In granting indulgences a proportionate cause is always necessary for the validity of the indulgence.[73] In a concession of this kind the Holy Father dispenses the merits of Christ. The Pope is not the master of these merits, and therefore must always have a reasonable cause to grant an indulgence.

(*b*) *For the liceity of a privilege.* A word will suffice to explain the necessity of a proportionate cause for the liceity of a privilege. Justice must rule in a society, and consequently everything which would savor of caprice must be avoided. Without a proportionate cause a privilege granted contrary to the law would injure justice. A privilege granted beyond the law without a reasonable cause would render the legislator guilty of undue favoritism.

The legislator, or Superior must clearly intend the particular good of the grantee.[74] But as this redounds to the common good he must also consider this aspect. Various reasons might be suggested, *e. g.*, desire to foster religion, utility, rewarding special service, etc.[75]

### 8. *Writing not essential to a privilege.*

Is it necessary for validity that a privilege be conferred in writing? The question is restricted to those privileges which have their origin in the direct concession of the legislator. Proper proof of a privilege does

---

71 Reiffenstuel, *o.c.*, lib. V, tit. XXXIII, n. 36.
72 Pirhing, *Ius Canonicum*, (Dillingae, 1674), lib. V, tit. XXXIII, n. 12.
73 Aertnys-Damen, *Theologia Moralis*, (Buscoduci, 1919), v. II, n. 1113.
74 Herincx, *o.c.*, tr. 3, disp. 4, q. 4, n. 62.
75 C. 15, 17, C. I, q. 7; c. 24, C. XXIII, q. 4.

not enter into the question. Only the essential influence of writing is considered.

Suarez[76] says that writing does not enter the substance of a privilege. He advances two reasons: first, there is no positive law which requires a document; second, because of the nature of the case the will of the legislator suffices. Suarez's second reason, is the proper juridical explanation for the non-necessity of a document.

Reiffenstuel,[77] Schmalzgrueber,[78] and Pirhing[79] make very light of the question of writing relative to the validity of a privilege. All three agree that the will of the legislator is sufficient.

Opposed to this argument are two texts of *Corpus Iuris* which apparently suggest the necessity of writing relative to the validity of a privilege.

Innocent IV wrote: *Postquam semel omnes provinciae suae dioceses visitaverint, licitum sit ei postea, prius tamen suffraganeorum suorum requisito consilio, et ipsius deffinitione super hoc habita coram eis, (quae in scripto esse volumus, ut possint aliis esse nota,)* ********* *opportunum.*[80] Alexander III wrote to the Bishop of Amiens: *Porro, quamvis Templarii et Hospitalarii multa sint libertatis praerogativa donati, non dubitamus, quin aliam libertatem habeat in locis, in quibus, antequam pervenisset ad eos, fuerant habitatores quod totum ex inspectione privilegiorum suorum plenius advertere potes, et secundum quod inveneris, ita observes. Sic enim eos volumus privilegiorum servare tenorem, quod eorum meta transgredi minime videantur.*[81]

---

76 Suarez, *o.c.*, lib. VIII, c. 2, n. 2.
77 Reiffenstuel, *o.c.*, lib. V, tit. XXXIII, n. 28.
78 Schmalzgrueber, *o.c.*, lib. V, tit. XXXIII, n. 14.
79 Pirhing, *o.c.*, lib. V, tit. XXXIII, n. 4.
80 C. 1, *de censibus, exactionibus, et procurationibus*, III, 20 in VI.
81 C. 7, X, *de privilegiis et excessibus privilegiatorum*, V, 33.

Suarez takes up these texts and shows that the question agitated was concerning the proof of the privilege. Very properly Suarez says that it is not permitted to infer that writing is necessary for the substance of a privilege. The two concepts are plainly different and from different things an inference has no place. At most Suarez admits a necessity *non simpliciter sed ad melius esse.*[82] Prescription of a Superior, however, may make a document necessary in particular cases.

9. *Must a Privilege be promulgated?*

Promulgation is the publication of a law by the competent authority.[83] Its purpose is to induce knowledge of a law and engender an obligation in respect to its observance. Promulgation differs from divulgation: the latter is diffusion of knowledge concerning the law. In all law promulgation is necessary. This necessity is founded upon the very idea of a law which is supposed to be a rule, or norm of human acts. Hence this rule must be known, or at least published in order to obtain its purpose.[84]

With this in mind, privileges in the wide sense, *e. g.*, clerical privileges, require promulgation. These privileges are real laws. Consequently they follow the necessity of laws. Now such laws contain a concession either as its substance, or as an accessory. In the first case, the privilege must be promulgated, not because it is privilege, but because it is a law. In the second case, the accessory follows the principal item. Since the latter is promulgated, the accessory is promulgated with it.[85]

On the other hand, it is easy to see that canonical promulgation has no place in privileges strictly so called.

---

82 Suarez, *o.c.*, lib. VIII, c. 2, n. 3.
83 Wernz, *o.c.*, v. I, n. 100.
84 C. 3, D. IV; Aertnys-Damen, *o.c.*, v. I, n. 144; Blat, *o.c.*, v. I, n. 64.
85 Suarez, *o.c.*, lib. VIII, c. 14, n. 6-7.

Yet ordinarily some modification is necessary, both in regard to the grantee himself, and in regard to others who must respect the use of the privilege.

The notice which should come to the grantee can take any form whatsoever. But absolute validity does not demand this notice. The legislator can, without any notice, or acceptance on the part of the grantee, concede him a privilege. The laws themselves were made by the legislator, or his predecessors and he has entire control over them. Yet strict privileges will usually contain the condition *si privilegium sibi concessum acceptet.*[86] Proper government demands that favors be accepted and in order to be accepted they must first be known.

Notification of a privilege to interested parties who must respect the legitimate use of the concession can take place at any time at all. No solemn promulgation is necessary. Practically speaking, this notification will become the proof of a privilege, and it will be considered in the chapter dealing with the proof of a privilege.

### 10. *Difference between Privileges and other Canonical Institutes.*

A. The differences between a law and a privilege have been noticed thruout this chapter. But in order to have these differences in one place, they will be repeated here.[87]

A privilege and a law differ in the following manner: (a) a law is made for a community; a privilege is granted to individual persons, or to classes of persons: (b) a

86 Schmalzgrueber, *o.c.*, lib. V, tit. XXXIII, n. 24; Can. 37 proposes the doctrine to be held concerning the validity of rescripts before acceptance; *Rescriptum impetrari potest pro alio etiam praeter eius assensum; et licet ipse possit gratia per rescriptum concessa non uti, rescriptum tamen valet ante eius acceptationem, nisi aliud ex appositis clausulis appareat.*

87 Herincx, *o.c.*, tr. 3, disp. 4, q. 4, n. 53; Grandclaude, *o.c.*, lib. V, tit. XXXIII, n. 1; Humphrey, *Conscience and Law*, (London, 1896), p. 163; Maroto, *o.c.*, v. I, n. 292; Cocchi, *o.c.*, v. I, n. 114.

law of its nature is perpetual; a privilege is not always perpetual: (c) a law must be promulgated; a privilege need not be promulgated: (d) a law consults the common good; a privilege consults the particular good; (e) a law has binding force; a privilege ordinarily has no binding force: (f) a law may deal also with penalties; a privilege considers only favors.

B. A dispensation is a relaxation of the law in a particular case.[88] A dispensation differs from a privilege in the following manner:[89] (a) a dispensation is always against the law; a privilege may also be outside of the law; (b) a dispensation is frequently granted for a single act; a privilege always implies a number of acts even when it is given *ad tempus;* (c) a dispensation often removes an obstacle which would hinder an act according to law, as in the case of a dispensation from an irregularity; a privilege permits a person to act contrary to the law, or beyond it; (d) a dispensation concerns a fact; a privilege is a norm of action.

C. A rescript is a written answer to a petition. A rescript differs from a privilege in several ways:[90] (a) a rescript is the document itself; a privilege is the favor contained in the document; (b) a rescript contains the interpretation of a law, or a dispensation, or a favor; a privilege is limited to a favor; (c) in general, a rescript refers to the form of a concession; a privilege is the concession itself.

---

88 Can. 80. *Dispensatio, seu legis in casu speciali relaxatio, concedi potest a conditore legis, ab eius successore vel Superiore, nec non ab illo cui iidem facultatem dispensandi concesserint.*

89 Herincx, *o.c., l.c.,* n. 54; Sanchez, *De Sancto Matrimonio Sacramento,* (Antwerpiae, 1626), lib. VIII, disp. I, n. 1; Zallinger, *Institutiones Iuris Ecclesiastici,* (Romae, 1832), lib. V, tit. XXXIII, § 263; Genicot, *Institutiones Theologiae Moralis,* (Bruxellis, 1922), 9 et 10 ed., v. I, n. 144; Humphrey, *o.c.,* p. 164; Sanguineti, *o.c.,* p. 72; Bargilliat, *Praelectiones Iuris Canonici,* (Parisiis, 1918), v. I, n. 100.

90 Palao, *Opus Morale,* (Lugduni, 1682), tr. III, disp. IV, p. I, n. 5; Grandclaude, *o.c.,* lib. V, tit. XXXIII, n. 1; Maroto, *o.c.,* v. I, n. 292; Cocchi, *o.c.,* v. I, n. 114.

D. *Gratia*, or *beneficium principis* differs from a privilege in several ways:[91] (a) every privilege is *gratia* in one form or another; but not every *gratia* is a privilege: (b) *gratia* is a concession in itself, e. g., benefice, or office; a privilege is a right to perform some action, or to omit performing some action: (c) *gratia* is a favor granted beyond the law; a privilege may also be contrary to the law.

---

91 Palao, *o.c.*, l.c., Devoti, *Institutiones Canonicae*, (Romae, 1825), v. I, c. III, § 36; Tamburini, *Opera Omnia*, (Venetiis, 1702), v. II, p. 317; St. Alphonsus, *Theologia Moralis*, (Augustae Taurinorum, 1879), lib. I, app. II, c. I, n. 1; Maroto, *o.c.*, l.c.; Cocchi, *o.c.*, l.c.

## CHAPTER II

## AUTHOR, SUBJECT, AND OBJECT OF A PRIVILEGE.

As the successor of Saint Peter, the Pope possesses the plenitude of power in all ecclesiastical matters.[1] The Bishops succeed the College of Apostles.[2] The personal prerogatives of the Apostles were not communicated to the Bishops. Thus the succession of the Bishops is perfect only when they act in unison as, for instance, in ecumenical councils. Nevertheless the power of the keys (*potestas clavium*), as the power derived from the Apostles is called, resides in both Pope and Bishops; in the former as pastor with universal jurisdiction,[3] and in the latter as pastors with particular jurisdiction.[4] Zallinger expresses the idea well: *Claves a Christo datae sunt uni, et datae sunt unitati.*[5]

The Pope and Bishops are legislators with the power of binding in conscience.[6] Since they are the founders of their law, it follows that they can exempt from it.[7]

---

1 For dogmatic proof cf. Conc. Vat., Const. (*Pastor Aeternus*), c. 3; Bellarminus, *Opera Omnia,* (Neapoli, 1872), v. I, lib. IV, c. XII-XVIII; Pesch, *Praelectiones Dogmaticae,* (Friburgi Brisgoviae, 1924), v. I, n. 464, 477-503. Cf. also Bacchinius, *Dissertatio de Ecclesiasticae Hierarchiae Originibus,* (Mutinae, 1703), pars I, c. III, n. 4, 25; Nannetti, *Brevi Nozioni di Diritto Publico Ecclesiastico,* (Bologna, 1840), v. I, pars II, § LVII, LIX.

2 For dogmatic proof cf. Conc. Tridentinum, sess. XXIII, *de ordine,* c. 4, can. 8; Pesch, *o.c.,* v. I, n. 433, 441; Cf. also Bargilliat, *Praelectiones Iuris Canonici,* (Parisiis, 1918), v. I, n. 587.

3 John c. 21, 15-17.

4 Bargilliat, *o.c.,* v. I, n. 594.

5 Zallinger, *Institutiones Iuris Naturalis et Eccl. Publici,* (Romae, 1823), lib. V, CCCLIX.

6 Cardenas, *Crisis Theologica,* (Venetiis, 1700), disp. XXII, c. 2-5; Bouquillon, *Theologia Moralis Fundamentalis,* (Brugis, 1890), n. 97.

7 Vecchiotti, *Institutiones Canonicae,* (Taurini, 1867), lib. II, c. II, 14, 20.

Hence, the power to grant privileges, at least those contrary to the law, resides in the legislators.[8] Evidently the utility of a strictly ecclesiastical law is in some way subject to circumstances. These circumstances may vary, and thus a complete revocation, or abrogation, would be necessary. In the same way, an individual good may be served without serious injury to the common good. This would give rise to either a dispensation, or to a privilege contrary to the law. If a legislator can abrogate a law, *a fortiore*, he can grant individual exemptions, or privileges.

### 1. *Authors of Privilege.*

THE POPE. In ecclesiastical matters the principal legislator is the Pope. His power is not subject to human limitations.[9] His jurisdiction is universal.[10] Hostiensis[11] and Suarez[12] paraphrase the words of Innocent III thus: *Privilegium Pontificis esse generale et divinum, ab illo autem manasse omnia canonica instituta.*[13] Both these writers interpret the word *privilegium* in this citation to mean supreme authority, but Suarez adds that this refers to spiritual jurisdiction. Yet besides this power in strictly spiritual matters, the Pope can grant a mixed privilege in two ways: first, in regard to temporal things which indirectly become spiritual, and, second, in purely temporal things with a view to a spiritual

---

8 Ballerini-Palmieri, *Opus Theologicum Morale,* (Prati, 1889), v. I, n. 388.

9 The Pope cannot grant a dispensation, or a privilege in matters of divine law. Thus the Pope cannot dispense from the impediment of "ligamen." Cf. Aertnys-Damen, *Theologia Moralis,* (Buscoduci, 1919), v. II, n. 772; Cappello, *De Sacramentis,* (Taurinorum Augustae, 1923), v. III, n. 224.

10 Can. 218; Brys, *o.c.*, p. 77.

11 Hostiensis, *o.c.,* lib. V, l.c.

12 Suarez, *o.c.,* lib. VIII, c. 8, n. 7.

13 *Quum ex illo generali privilegio, quod beato Petro et per eum ecclesiae Romanae Dominus noster indulsit, canonica postmodum manaverint instituta,* ******** *de iure pertineant.* C. 1, X, *de translatione Episcopi,* I, 7.

purpose. Thus tithes as well as legitimation can become the object of a privilege.[14]

The Pope cannot grant a privilege when it would be contrary to his own dignity.[15] However, he can concede favors where his dignity is not infringed: e. g., giving others the right to fill benefices which otherwise would belong to him.

The Pope can grant privileges beyond the law provided he has dominion over the object of the privilege.

Altho the power to grant privileges resides in the Pope, it is not necessary for him to exercise this power personally. This power can be delegated. In fact, the Congregations of the Roman Curia are the usual channels thru which the Pope concedes his favors.[16]

Bishops. Besides the Pope, Bishops enjoy ordinary power to make laws.[17] Their jurisdiction, however, is confined to the territory which has been assigned to their care.[18] Bishops, therefore, cannot grant privileges which are contrary to the common law of the Church.[19] This power, however, may be enjoyed thru delegation. Nor can Bishops grant privileges contrary to the laws of a provincial, or plenary council. In these councils the individual Bishop is only one of the legislators,[20] and consequently he has not entire control of the law. In common law the Code recognizes the power of dispensation[21] but postulates a just cause without which the dispensation would be invalid. In particular law the Code concedes the power of dispensation, but it does not concede the power of granting privileges.[22]

---

14 Suarez, *o.c.*, *l.c.*
15 Suarez, *o.c.*, *lib.* VIII, c. 8, n. 8.
16 Can. 7, 247-258.
17 Can. 329, § 1; Suarez, *o.c.*, lib. VIII, c. 8, n. 9.
18 Demeuron, *L'Eglise*, (Paris, 1914), p. 76, 123.
19 Wernz, *o.c.*, v. I, n. 159, 1; Cocchi, *o.c.*, v. I, n. 116.
20 S.C.S. Off., Sept. 10, 1896, Coll. n. 1952.
21 Can. 81, 84.
22 Can. 291, § 2.

Contrary to his own laws, a Bishop enjoys the power of granting a privilege. In these laws the Bishop is the sole legislator,[23] and has entire control over the laws.[24]

Outside the field of his own law, a Bishop can grant a privilege provided the object of the privilege is not already forbidden in some way in common law, and provided the Bishop has dominion over the object of the privilege. Therefore, Bishops cannot grant habitual faculties since they themselves do not enjoy these faculties.[25]

VICARS, AND PREFECTS APOSTOLIC. Ordinary power is also enjoyed by Vicars and Prefects Apostolic.[26] Their power to grant privileges is the same as that of the Bishops.

APOSTOLIC ADMINISTRATORS PERMANENTER CONSTITUTI. According to the Code,[27] the power of the permanently assigned Apostolic Administrators is the same as the power of the Bishops. Hence their competence in the field of privilege is similar to the power of the Bishops.

ABBOTS AND PRELATES NULLIUS. Abbots, and Prelates *nullius* also possess ordinary jurisdiction.[28] Hence they, too, are competent to grant privileges contrary to their own laws. But they cannot concede privileges contrary to the laws of the provincial, or plenary council in which they must take part.[29]

RELIGIOUS SUPERIORS AND CHAPTERS. By disposition of law,[30] religious Superiors and Chapters in exempt clerical institutes have the power of jurisdiction. Since

23 Can. 362.
24 Craisson, *Manuale totius Iuris Canonici,* (Pictavii, 1875), 4 ed., v. I, n. 161.
25 Wernz, *o.c.*, v. I, n. 159, ad calcem 25.
26 Can. 294, § 1.
27 Can. 315, § 1.
28 Can. 323, § 1.
29 Can. 285, 291, § 2.
30 Can. 501, § 1.

both the religious Superiors and the Chapters are legislators, they can concede privileges contrary to their laws unless forbidden by their constitutions.

In addition to their ordinary power of granting privileges in the matters of their own laws, Ordinaries may concede privileges by reason of delegation, or by reason of vicarious power. Thus Bishops, Abbots, or Prelates *nullius*, Vicars, and Prefects Apostolic, and major Superiors of exempt clerical religious enjoy the power of declaring an altar privileged.[31]

Briefly, the power of Superiors to grant privileges can be gathered from these simple rules: (a) the Pope is competent in all laws, general or particular, no matter whether the laws are made by himself, or by an ecumenical council, or by a predecessor, or by an inferior legislator; (b) a Bishop, or a Prelate with ordinary jurisdiction is competent merely in the laws made by himself, or by his predecessor;[32] (c) Privileges beyond the law can be granted by Superiors provided they have dominion over the object of the privilege. All Prelates inferior to the Pope cannot grant a privilege beyond the law should the object of the privilege be forbidden in some way in common law.

## 2. *Subject, and Object of a Privilege.*

Subject of a Privilege. The subject of a privilege contrary to the law, must be one who is first under obedience to the law itself.[33] Since this kind of a privilege exempts from the obligation arising from the law, it is necessary that an obligation should first exist else there can be no exemption from it.[34] Privileges beyond the

---

31 Can. 916.

32 Bargilliat, *o.c.*, v. I, n. 102; Ayrinhac, *General Legislation in the New Code of Canon Law,* (New York, 1923), n. 157.

33 Hostiensis, *o.c., de privilegiis et excessibus privilegiatorum*, n. 7.

34 Cocchi, *o.c.*, v. I, n. 116; Maroto, *Institutiones Iuris Canonici,* 3 ed., (Romae, 1921), v. I, n. 296.

law, however, can be conceded to non-subjects of the law.[35] But the matter of the privilege beyond the law, even if it is conceded to a non-subject of the law, must be included in matter over which the legislator has control, and concerning which he can force respect for the privilege. Jurisdiction is not necessary in conceding privileges beyond the law.[36]

OBJECT OF A PRIVILEGE. A privilege should be just, reasonable, and honest.[37] Anything, then, which fulfills these three requisites, can become the object of a privilege. Primarily this is true of privileges contrary to the law. Besides, the object of a privilege must contain a special favor.[38] Lastly, the concession should usually be permanent in accordance with the principle *decet concessum a principe beneficium esse mansurum.*[39]

---

35 Makee, *o.c.*, v. I, n. 319.
36 Wernz, *o.c.*, v. I, n. 159, 2.
37 Suarez, *o.c.*, lib. VIII, c. 9, n. 1.
38 C. 25, X, *de verborum significatione*, V, 40, *nec esset privata (lex) nisi aliquid specialiter indulgeret.*
39 R.J. 16 in VI; Can. 70. *Privilegium, nisi aliud constet, censendum est perpetuum.*

## CHAPTER III

## DIVISION OF PRIVILEGES.

Before entering upon the various divisions of privileges as found in commentaries published after the promulgation of the Code,[1] it will be interesting to see how, in a few bold strokes, one author grouped all privileges. The Jesuit Tamburini, who wrote more than two centuries ago, prefixed this division of privileges to his commentary on the *Bulla Cruciatae*.

Privileges, says Tamburini, are personal, real, or mixed.[2] Mixed privileges accrue to individual persons by reason of age or condition. Real privileges are connected with places or certain kinds of actions. Personal privileges, however, are conceded to individual persons, either because of their own merit, or because they happen to be members of a privileged community. The last-named subdivision is called a corporal privilege. It can be further subdivided in privileges which all the members, as individual persons, can enjoy, and privileges which are enjoyed only when the community acts as a unit.

This scheme of division proposed by Tamburini, is useful enough to obtain a general view of the several classifications of privileges, but its utility scarcely goes beyond generalities. Both strict and non-strict privileges can be fitted into the parts of the entire scheme. While

---

1 Maroto, *Institutiones Iuris Canonici*, (Romae, 1921) 3rd edition, v. I, n. 293; Vermeersch-Creusen, *o.c.*, v. I, n. 129; Blat, *Commentarium in textum Codicis Iuris Canonici*, (Romae, 1921), v. I, n. 133; Augustine, *A Commentary on the New Code of Canon Law*, (St. Louis, 1921) 4th edition, v. I, p. 153; Ayrinhac, *General Legislation in the New Code of Canon Law*, (New York, 1923) n. 115.

2 Tamburini, *Opera Omnia*, (Venetiis, 1702), v. II, p. 317.

this same objection is valid, in a certain sense, against the divisions proposed by modern authors, yet it loses much of its force from the clear line of demarcation between those privileges which are particular concessions, and the privileges which are properly speaking laws containing a favor. Once this necessary distinction is made, and properly understood, no difficulty will arise concerning the nature, interpretation, and use of the privileges found in the various divisions.

Divisions of Privileges. 1. The first division of privileges is sought in the source of the concession. According to this division, privileges *strictly* so-called are concessions embodying a favor. In an *efficient* sense, it is the provision itself which is called a privilege, but in a *subjective* sense, the privilege is the favor contained in the grant. These privileges are not laws, altho, by analogy, they are frequently described as favorable laws.[3] On the other hand, privileges *widely* so-called are real laws. They too, in an *efficient* sense, are the laws themselves, while in a *subjective* sense, the privileges are the favors contained in the laws.[4] Thus in the new Code are enumerated the privileges of clerics,[5] of religious,[6] and of novices.[7]

Besides these widely so-called privileges of the new Code, such privileges can also exist in particular law. An example of such a privilege would be a particular form of election, different from the method described in the Code.[8] Privileges coming under this subdivision must be carefully distinguished from strict privileges

---

3 E. g., Wernz, *o.c.*, v. I, n. 158, II; Maroto, *o.c.*, v. I, n. 291; Blat, *o.c.*, v. I, n. 129; Augustine, *o.c.*, v. I, p. 152; Ayrinhac, *o.c.*, n. 154-155.

4 Maroto, *o.c.*, v. I, n. 293.

5 Can. 119-122.

6 Can. 615.

7 Can. 567, § 1.

8 Can. 161-178.

since the latter likewise are outside the field of common law.

Another point must be emphasized here. It is necessary to keep in mind the notions of the foregoing division because the mere classification of a privilege will not always reveal whether or not it is a strict privilege; the favor may, perhaps, merely emanate from a favorable common, or particular law.

2. Privileges are divided into privileges *contrary to the law,* (*contra ius*) and privileges *beyond the law* (*praeter ius*). The first class argues an exemption from the common, or particular law. As observed above,[9] the concession of such a privilege postulates the power of jurisdiction. This jurisdictional power must be universal, or regional, according to the scope of the law contrary to which the privilege is granted. Therefore the Pope is competent in all ecclesiastical law; but a Bishop's competence is limited to his own laws. A privilege *beyond the law* is a mere favor which does not injure a law. All that is required to grant such a privilege is dominion, or at least, as in the case of indulgences, the power of dispensation.[10] *Privilegia secundum ius* are not proper privileges because no precise concession is made.[11]

3. Privileges can be *personal* (*personale*), or *real* (*reale*). A *personal* privilege is conceded directly in favor of a person. A *real* privilege adheres to some dignity, place, or duty.

*Personal* privileges are subdivided into *individually* (*singulariter*) *personal, commonly* (*communiter*) *personal,* and *corporal* (*corporale*) privileges.[12] An *indi-*

---

9 Cf. p. 28.

10 The Holy Father is the dispenser, not the master, of the treasury of the merits of Christ existing in the Church. Aertnys-Damen, *Theologia Moralis,* (Buscoduci, 1920), v. II, n. 1113.

11 Wernz, *o.c.,* v. I, n. 158, ad calcem 12.

12 Maroto, *o.c.,* v. I, n. 293.

*vidually personal* privilege is one which is granted to a physical person, entirely because of his own merits. The privilege of a portable altar in favor of a priest would be such a privilege. A *commonly personal* privilege is one granted to physical person because he belongs to a certain state, or possesses a certain dignity. Such are the privileges of Cardinals,[13] Bishops,[14] patrons,[15] etc. A *corporal* privilege is one conceded to a moral person. All the members of this moral person usually enjoy the privilege but only by reason of their association with the moral person.[16]

*Real* privileges are likewise subdivided.[17] Real privileges are called *local,* (*locale*) if the privilege is granted to a place: *muneral* (*munus, munerale*), if granted to a dignity, or office: and properly *real* (*res, reale*), if granted to tangible things. This last-named class will include the *real* privileges not distinctly local, or muneral. All real privileges continue even if the physical beneficiary is not at hand to enjoy them.

There are several ways to determine whether a privilege is *personal* or *real.*[18] First, the wording of the grant itself will very frequently decide the issue. The object of the privilege may also aid in dispelling a doubt. Similarly, the character of the person who receives the grant may help to solve a doubt. But, if, after using

---

13 Can. 239.

14 Can. 349.

15 Can. 1455.

16 It is important to know whether a privilege is individually or commonly personal, or corporal. The first ceases with the death of the grantee (Can. 74). The second likewise, as far as the immediate beneficiary is concerned, ceases with the beneficiary, but the privileges themselves continue in the dignity, or office. A corporal privilege continues for another hundred years after the death of the immediate physical beneficiaries. This, of course, supposes that the corporal privileges were not granted for a specified time, and that the moral person continues to exist according to the provision of canon 102.

17 De Meester, *Compendium Iuris Canonici et Iuris Canonico-Civilis,* (Brugis, 1921), n. 305; Raus, *Institutiones Canonicae,* (Lugduni-Parisiis, 1923), n. 40, I.

these criterions, a doubt still remains, the principle of Sexto Bonifacii VIII[19] can be applied. *Odia restringi, et favores convenit ampliari.* This will mean that a *favorable* privilege can be considered *real,* and an *odious* privilege *personal.*[20]

4. Privileges can be *favorable* (*favorabile*), or *odious* (*odiosum*). A *favorable* privilege contains a favor without causing diminution of the rights of a third party. Thus the privilege of an indulgenced altar is a favorable privilege since no loss, or curtailment of rights results from the use of the privilege. An *odious* privilege, however, contains a favor, but at the same time it diminishes the rights of a third person. Exemption from tithes would be such a privilege. It is evident that an *odious* privilege is simultaneously both favorable and odious; the former in respect of the grantee, the latter in respect of interested parties. The reason of the division of privileges into favorable, and odious privileges is sought in the absence, or presence of prejudice to rights of third parties.

5. Privileges can be *affirmative* (*affirmativum*), or *negative* (*negativum*).[21] An *affirmative* privilege provides the faculty to perform some action otherwise unlawful. Thus the faculty to absolve from reserved sins, to celebrate certain votive, or proper masses, to bestow special blessings, etc., are all affirmative privileges. A *negative* privilege, on the other hand, concedes an exemption from an act demanded by law. Such a grant would be the privilege not to fast on the days required by law.

6. Privileges can be *gracious* (*gratiosum*), *remu-*

---

18 Cocchi, *Commentarium in Codicem Iuris Canonici,* (Taurinorum Augustae, 1921), v. I, p. 184, scholion; Maroto, *o.c.,* l.c.

19 R. J. 15 in VI.

20 Zoesius, *Commentarium in Ius Canonicum Universum,* (Venetiis, 1757), lib. V, tit. XXXIII, n. 6.

21 Raus, *o.c.,* l.c.

*nerative* (*remunerativum*), or *onerous* (*onerosum*). A *gracious* privilege finds its source in the pure liberality of a Superior. No precise attention is paid to the merits of the grantee. This does not mean that the Superior must not consider the worth of the person he desires to enrich with a privilege, but rather that the worth of the privileged person is not considered as a determining motive in granting the privilege. A *remunerative* privilege is granted in view of some particular merit, or in gratitude for the performance of some special service. In these cases the worth of the grantee has a direct influence on the benevolence of his Superior. Signal service in the interest of the Church may be thus rewarded. An *onerous* privilege has its foundation in justice. It is given in return for a burden assumed. This kind of a privilege will frequently be found in concordats.

Maroto[22] records a special division of *privilegium purum*, and *privilegium conventionale*. Conceding that there is some difference between this division and the division of privileges into gracious, remunerative and onerous privileges, nevertheless Maroto's division can be reduced to the division explained in the preceding paragraph. *Privilegium purum* is one which is granted without any contract, or any kind of mutual obligation. Hence it is practically a *gracious* privilege, altho it may, possibly, tend toward the notion of a *remunerative* privilege. *Privilegium conventionale* is founded upon reciprocal obligation. It will differ from an *onerous* privilege in this that it implies a public and explicit agreement.

7. Privileges can be *absolute* (*absolutum*), *conditional* (*conditionale*), or *modal* (*modale*). An *absolute* privilege is granted without any conditions. Thus, if the Holy Father should grant a priest the privilege of saying mass in a private oratory, without stipulating any condi-

---

22 Maroto, *o.c.*, l.c.

tions, the grantee would enjoy an absolute privilege, and he could use his privilege even if it were convenient to celebrate mass in a church. A *conditional* privilege has effect only when the conditions under which the privilege was conceded are fulfilled. Therefore such a privilege cannot be used irrespective of the stipulations of the grant because the Superior's consent is not obtained if the conditions are not fulfilled. The existence of a condition in a privilege, aside from its presence in the rescript, can often be learned from the object of the privilege. Thus a blind priest who enjoys the privilege of celebrating mass, cannot use this privilege if the assistance of another priest, or deacon cannot be obtained. A *modal* privilege concerns the manner in which the faculty conceded by the privilege may be exercised. Such a privilege is likewise restricted to the stipulations found in the rescript. In effect a modal privilege is practically the same as a conditional privilege.

8. Privileges can be divided according to the manner in which they were conceded. Thus privileges are called *motu proprio,* or *ad instantiam.* The former is granted without any reference to a petition even if some favor had been requested of a Superior. A privilege conceded *ad instantiam* is given in compliance with a petition. Should no petition of any kind be made, it is clear that the privilege is granted *motu proprio.* But if some petition were directed to the proper Superior, the rescript will have to be examined in order to learn whether the grant is in compliance with the petition, or conceded independently of it.

9. The manner of acquisition furnishes another point of division of privileges. The various methods of obtaining a privilege will be treated at length in a later chapter.[23] At present it is sufficient to mention that

23 Cf. ch. IV.

according to this point of division, privileges are acquired by *direct concession, communication, custom,* and *prescription.*

10. Privileges can be *written* (*scriptum*), or *non-written* (*non-scriptum*). The former is obtained by means of a rescript: the latter may be acquired in three ways: (a) *orally,* as, for instance, in an audience with the Holy Father; (b) by *custom,* when the community acting as a unit fulfills the requirements of canons 25-27;[24] (c) by *prescription,* when an individual person obtains a right according to the provisions of law.[25]

11. Privileges can be *temporary* (*temporale*), or *perpetual* (*perpetuum*). A *temporary* privilege is confined to the limits of the time determined in the grant. This limit of time may be expressed in terms of months, or years, or even according to the number of cases. An individually personal privilege is always a temporary privilege, because at most it is limited to the life of the grantee. In other privileges, the phrase *ad beneplacitum meum,* or its equivalent, will indicate the temporary character of the privilege. A *perpetual* privilege is one which is conceded without limit of time. Corporal, and real privileges are of such a character, provided they adhere to a moral person, dignity, or thing of itself perpetual. According to canon 70 a privilege is perpetual unless the contrary is evident. Hence the limitation of time must be proved.[26]

12. Finally, privileges can be *private* (*privatum*), or *common* (*commune*). A *private* privilege goes no farther than to consult the benefit accruing to an individual person. It matters little whether, in point of fact, several persons enjoy the same privilege as long as the privilege is concerned with the individual convenience, and not with the welfare of the persons considered as a unit.

---

24 Cf. ch. IV.

25 Raus, *o.c.,* l.c., cf. p. 66.

26 Maroto, *o.c.,* l.c.

Therefore, an entire community may enjoy a *private* privilege. All that is necessary is that the accruing benefit be found directly in the members of the community. A *common* privilege, on the other hand, is granted for the common good. Such a privilege would be conceded to a community, a class of persons, or an assembly. The privilege is considered as directly affecting the association rather than its members. Individual members of such an association receive the benefit of a *common* privilege, but in no way does the privilege become their individual right. Hence, individual members cannot renounce their association's common privileges.[27] Faculties of dispensation, and privileges of precedence vested in a community, or assembly are examples of a common privilege.

27 Cf. p. 113.

## CHAPTER IV

## ACQUISITION OF PRIVILEGES.

The Code enumerates four ways in which a privilege can be acquired. These methods are *direct concession, communication, custom* and *prescription.* The latter two have much in common, but for the sake of clarity they will considered separately.

**Can. 63. § 1. Privilegia acquiri possunt non solum per directam concessionem competentis auctoritatis et per communicationem, sed etiam per legitimam consuetudinem aut praescriptionem.**

### 1. *Direct Concession of Privileges.*

Direct concession is the principal method of obtaining a privilege.[1] This concession is twofold. The legislator, or competent authority may accede to the petition of one of his subjects, or he may confer the privilege entirely of his own volition, and for reasons known to himself. The former concession is known as *ad instantiam* and the latter is called *motu proprio.*

As observed above, the legislator is no wise obliged to commit his favors to writing.[2] Every concession has its source in the benevolent will of a Superior irrespective of the public disposition made of the concession. This is true even from the nature of the case but *Corpus Iuris* is not silent on the point. Paul II expressly states that concessions are made both orally and by document.[3]

---

1 Ayrinhac, *o.c.*, n. 157; Santi, *Praelectiones Iuris Canonici*, (Ratisbonae, 1886), lib. V, tit. XXXIII, n. 5.

2 Cf. p. 18.

3 C. 3 *de penitentiis et remissionibus*, V, 9 in Extra. Com.

From this it does not follow that a privilege granted orally has the same probative force as one set down in a document.[4]

*Confirmation* of a privilege is allied to concession. Altho confirmation differs from concession in this that it supposes a privilege to exist, while the latter produces the privilege, yet in some cases confirmation of a privilege is not more than a mere recognition of a former privilege. Should this obtain, confirmation leaves the privilege with all the defects it may possibly have. It would not validate them.[5] Such confirmation of a privilege is called *in forma communi.*[6]

Another form of confirmation removes possible defects. This form is called *in forma speciali.*[7] An examination of the former privilege is presupposed in this form of confirmation. Practically it amounts to a new concession.[8]

The extent of the confirmation accorded a privilege must be learned from the document. If the phrase *ex certa scientia* is present, the confirmation is in special form, because this phrase gives the same effect as if the legislator were to grant the concession entirely of his own will.[9] In order to have the same juridical effect, it is not absolutely necessary to use these words verbatim.[10] In case of a doubt concerning the value of confirmation of a privilege, the common form must be understood.[11] The presumption is that the legislator has not changed

4 Cf. p. 136.

5 Amort, *Elementa Iuris Canonici*, (Ferrariae, 1763), lib. V, tit. XXXIII, § 22.

6 C. 7, X, *de confirmatione utili vel inutili*, II, 30; c. 5, X, *de concessione praebendae et ecclesiae non vacantis*, III, 8; Suarez, *o.c.*, lib. VIII, c. 18, n. 3-4, 8; Sanguineti, *o.c.*, n. 140.

7 C. 8, X, *de confirmatione utili vel inutili*, II, 30; Suarez, *o.c.*, lib. VIII, c. 18, n. 5; Sanguineti, *o.c.*, l.c.

8 Suarez, *o.c.*, lib. VIII, c. 18, n. 12.

9 Barbosa, *Tractatus Varii*, (Lugduni, 1660), *De Clausulis Usufrequentioribus*, claus. LIX.

10 Suarez, *o.c.*, lib. VIII, c. 18, n. 6.

11 Sanguineti, *o.c.*, l.c.

his will. Consequently, possible revocation of a privilege in the past, all its defects, and restrictions remain in force unless the document embodying the confirmation of the privilege clearly shows that it has been granted *ex certa scientia*.

*Innovation,* or *renewal* (*innovatio*) of a privilege is almost the same as confirmation of a privilege. Either the document or the precise favor can be renewed.[12] One can be renewed without the other.[13] Renewal of the document will not be of great importance except in relation to proving a privilege. But renewal of the favor contained in the document enjoys some importance. This importance arises from the root-meaning of the word *innovatio* and its actual juridical usage. Etymologically, "to renew" means to give back, to restore, to return. Hence to renew a privilege would also mean a restoration of revoked privileges. But, save for the phrase *ex certa scientia,* this is not the fact. Renewal of a privilege merely confirms the privileges which have not been revoked.[14]

Renewal of a privilege can be *in common* or *in special form.* In the first instance, privileges remain in the same state as they were before renewal, while in the second case defects are removed.

Since privileges are very often conceded in the form of a rescript, it will be well to bear in mind a few fundamental notions concerning a rescript itself.[15]

The Roman emporers were often asked for an interpretation of a law. Their answer was known as *rescriptum.* Hence the word means a written answer to a petition. But since the answer came from one who had authority, the formal meaning of rescript is: *a written*

---

12 Reiffenstuel, *o.c.*, lib. V, tit. XXXIII, n. 76.

13 Suarez, *o.c.*, lib. VIII, c. 20, n. 4.

14 Suarez, *o.c.*, lib. VIII, c. 20, n. 1; Reiffenstuel, *o.c.*, lib. V, tit. XXXIII, n. 74.

15 Maroto, *o.c.*, V. I, n. 271.

*answer given by a prince, or by one in authority.*[16] The word *rescriptum* was taken up by the Roman Pontiffs. Wernz[17] points out that even before the time of Pope Siricius the word was in use. The word continued in favor, and from the time of Alexander III (1159-1180) we find many responses or *rescripta.* Bernard of Pavia wrote the first commentary on rescripts, and two centuries later the whole theory of rescripts and their use were perfected by the Rules of Apostolic Chancery. Finally with some change, especially concerning the subject of a rescript, the same title is found in the Code of Canon Law.[18]

During the law of the Decretals, anyone could ask for a rescript unless he were (a) a false or recalled procurator, (b) a heretic or schismatic, (c) an excommunicate.[19] Only the major excommunication was considered and this, too, in causes not connected with the same excommunication. An excommunicated person could file a petition in his own defense. On September 9, 1898, the Sacred Penitentiary said that rescripts of occult excommunicates were valid in the internal forum, provided they consisted of minor favors such as blessing rosaries, etc.[20] Pius X in his constitution *Sapienti Consilio* made no exceptions unless a person were excommunicated by name, or suspended *a divinis* by the Holy See.[21] The Code is even more generous. None at all are excepted: but the condition of excommunication, suspension, or personal interdict must be mentioned in the petition for a rescript.[22]

Besides acceding to the petition of one of his subjects, the legislator can grant a privilege *motu proprio.*

16 Maroto, *o.c., l.c.*
17 Wernz, *o.c.*, v. I, n. 149.
18 Can. 36-62.
19 C. 1, *de rescriptis*, I, 3 in VI.
20 In Wernz, *o.c.*, v. I, n. 151, ft. 30.
21 AAS. v. I, p. 64.
22 Can. 36; 2265, § 2; 2275, n. 2; 2283.

A concession of this kind is one in which the Superior is actuated by motives of his own, independently of any petition.[23] Such independent action does not signify that in no way at all was the matter brought to the Superior's attention, but it does mean that the favor was granted without reference to the petition, or for reasons other than the ones mentioned in the petition. In a word, in cases where some petition was made, the final cause is the legislator's will, and not the petition.

A privilege granted *motu proprio* validates a subreption (*subreptio*) or a suppression of truth, but it does not validate the proposal of a false cause, provided this cause were the only one mentioned.[24] The reason is that the suppression of truth may render the privilege indiscreet while the proposal of a false cause vitiates the benevolent will of the Superior.[25]

While it is true that the phrase *motu proprio* will validate a subreption, it must be borne in mind that this subreption must not be intrinsic, that is, it must not pertain to the inability of the subject who requests the favor. If the subreption were intrinsic, the privilege would not be valid,[26] unless a derogatory clause were added.

Similarly rescripts, even if granted *motu proprio*, cannot be sustained if the grant is contrary to legitimate custom, or a particular statute, or the rights of a third person. Derogatory clauses, however, can remove this disability.[27]

---

23 Palao, *o.c.*, tr. 3, disp. 4, p. 2, §6, n. 1.
24 Can. 45.
25 Palao, *o.c.*, l.c., n. 3.
26 Palao, *o.c.*, l.c., n. 7; Barbosa, *o.c.*, claus. LXXIX.
27 Can. 46.

## 2. *Communication of Privileges.*

### A. *Development and History of Communication of Privileges.*

Strictly speaking, the method of obtaining privileges by *communication*, pertained to religious Orders. But the word "communicatio" was used also in other concessions of privileges. Thus Urban VIII in his constitution, *Quoniam divinae*, June 1, 1627, communicated the privileges of the Roman schools to the new German College in Prague.[28] On the same day the Pope communicated the same privileges to the new German College in Vienna.[29] This form of communication of privileges was known as *ad instar*.

The possibility of such a privilege is clear from the consideration of the real cause of a privilege. The will of the legislator is the basis upon which all privileges rest. As far as validity is concerned, it matters little whether the terms of the privilege be defined in so many words, or conceded according to the favors of another grant. Innocent IV, while not using the term *ad instar* clearly refers to this kind of a privilege when he discusses the privileges of the students in Rome.[30]

A privilege *ad instar* was a norm according to which a later privilege was patterned. The second was an imitation of the first privilege, and it included all the favors which had been originally granted.[31] As long as the first concession remained the same, no diffiiculty in understanding the second privilege presented itself. But what if the initial concession were augmented? Did the second

28 Bull. Rom. tom. 13, p. 551.

29 Bull. Rom. tom. 13, p. 556.

30 C. 2, *de privilegiis et excessibus privilegiatorum*, V, 7 in VI; *Volumus et statuimus, ut studentes in scholis ipsis penes sedem eandem talibus privilegiis omnino, libertatibus et immunitatibus gaudeant, quibus gaudent studentes in scholis, ubi generale regitur studium, ac recipiant integre proventus suos ecclesiasticos sicut illi.*

31 Suarez, *o.c.*, lib. VIII, c. 15, n. 2.

privilege likewise receive this increase? To give an answer to these questions, it must be remembered that the second privilege is an imitation of the first, not merely as a model but with all its qualifications.[32] The aspect of model would appear in such a concession: We grant you a privilege as Paul enjoys. The aspect of qualification would be: We grant you Paul's privilege. From this it can be seen that only the external imitation is present in the first instance, while an intrinsic note is found in the second. Now this imitation exists primarily at the time when the second concession is made. From then on the two privileges are distinct, and bear relation to each other only in similitude. Both are self-existent and independent. Therefore what would accrue to the first would not benefit the second, and *vice versa.*[33]

But if the first privilege were invalid, no privilege at all would be conceded to the second grantee because the foundation for the concession would be lacking. Manifestly, should something be granted after the fashion of another privilege, but the latter be actually without validity, the former would be similarly invalid.[34]

Communication of privileges among the Orders was reserved for the reign of Leo X. Before that time and even before the beginning of sixteenth century instances of communication are at hand, but it was not the same rule that Leo X inaugurated. Sixtus IV in his constitution, *Sedis Apostolica,* May 27, 1474, communicated the privileges of the Mendicants to the Congregation of Saint Francis of Paul.[35] Alexander VI, in his constitution, *Ad ea,* May 1, 1501 likewise communicated privileges to the Minims.[36] A few years later, June 17, 1508, Julius II, in his constitution, *Etsi,* communicated the privileges

32 Palao, *o.c.,* tr. 3, disp. 4, p. 2, § 8, n. 4.
33 Suarez, *o.c.,* lib. VIII, c. 15, n. 3-5.
34 Suarez, *o.c.,* lib. VIII, c. 15, n. 6.
35 Bull. Rom. tom. 5, p. 213.
36 Bull. Rom. tom. 5, p. 381.

of the Mendicants to the Augustinians.[37] While these grants were called communication of privileges, they did not allow for a general exchange of privileges.

The principle of general exchange of privileges among the mendicant Orders was promulgated by Pope Leo X in his constitution, *Dudum,* December 10, 1519. The Pope writes: *Nos ad singulos Ordines******** motu proprio et ex mera nostra scientia et liberalitate, de apostolicae auctoritatis plenitudine communicavimus. Illaque omnia et singula inter dictorum Ordinum personas, pariformiter communia fuisse et esse volumus, prout in singulis litteris praedictis plenius continetur.*[38] The Orders named in this constitution are: Praedicatores, Minores, Eremitae S. Augustini, Carmelitae, Servi Beatae Mariae Virginis, and Minores fratres.

With this principle in force it was only a question of time before all Orders, whether mendicant or not, would exchange their privileges. Cognizant of the self-sacrificing and heroic work of all Orders, Pius V granted all of them equal consideration in the matter of concessions. Consequently, in his constitution of August 16, 1567, *Ex supernae,* Pius V laid down the more ample rule that all Orders henceforth would communicate their privileges.[39] In a later constitution, *Romani Pontificis,* June 30, 1570, Pius V made a reservation concerning the communication of privileges. This reservation was that privileges refering to temporalities would not be communicated.[40] This, of course, was eminently just, since the extreme poverty of the Mendicants did not obtain in the non-Mendicant Orders. The latter could more easily afford contributions and assessments. Therefore, unless the non-Mendicant Orders were individually exempted

---

37 Bull. Rom. tom. 5, p. 421.
38 Bull. Rom. tom. 5, p. 732.
39 Bull. Rom. tom. 7, p. 586.
40 Bull. Rom. tom. 7, p. 837.

from these payments, they enjoyed no privilege in this matter.

The word "communication" now had a new and a definite meaning. It meant that when one Order received a privilege, all the other Orders were by that very fact similarly privileged. Still the former use of the word was retained. Urban VIII employed it when he conceded the indults of the Congregation of Saint John of God to the Mendicant Orders.[41]

Clement VII did not amplify the concessions of his predecessors. In his constitutions he specifies the limits of the communication conceded. Thus he communicated the privileges of Conventuals and Camaldulese monks to the Cappuchins,[42] and the privileges of the monks of Saint Augustine to the *Jesuiti Fratres* of Saint Jerome.[43]

In communication of privileges, favors relating to Prelates were communicated to Prelates, convents to convents, feasts to feasts, etc. Julius II in his letter of June 1, 1509, to the Bishop of Cordova made this stipulation.[44] Latter-day communication of privileges retained this order. But personal privileges of individual religious were in no wise communicated to their associates in religion.[45] Similarly privileges conceded to a church or to an altar in honor of a certain saint were not subject to communication.[46] Thus the Portiuncula indulgence, while communicated to the churches of the Franciscan Order, did not obtain in the churches of the other Orders.

In conceding communication of privileges, the Supreme Pontiffs presupposed that the new privileges would not interfere with the regular observance of the rule existing in each Order. The reason for this is evident: the Pope intends to foster religion and not to

41 Bull. Rom. tom. 13, p. 169.
42 Bull. Rom. tom. 6, p. 113.
43 Bull. Rom. tom. 6, p. 158.
44 In Reiffenstuel, *o.c.*, lib. V, tit. XXXIII, n. 59.
45 Reiffenstuel, *o.c.*, lib. V, tit. XXXIII, n. 60.
46 Reiffenstuel, *o.c.*, lib. V, tit. XXXIII, n. 62.

weaken it in any way. Thus since it would have been against the rule of some Orders that members of the Order should act as witnesses in court, this item of the rule prevented them from participating in the privilege of giving testimony conceded to the military Orders.[47]

Before discussing the present terminology relative to communication of privileges, it is well to see what expressions were used by earlier canonists, and how these expressions can be blended to present day legislation.

Palao[48] mentions three ways of communication of privileges. The first is by aggregation, or by extension of the same privilege. No new concession is made, but more subjects are brought within the scope of one and the same privilege. The second manner obtains in including secondary persons in a privilege made to the principal grantee. In both of these instances the accessory follows the principal privilege. Therefore the accessory privilege increases, or decreases according to the fortunes of the principal privilege. The third method amounts really to a new concession of privilege, and is independent of the fortunes of the first privilege. Palao adds that the Jesuits could not use their own privileges, or the ones communicated to them unless the communication came thru the General of the Society. This was due to the Jesuit constitutions which make the entire government depend on the General. Other religious bodies were not similarly restricted.

Schmalzgrueber[49] says there are two ways to receive privileges by communication, but his ideas are really the same as those of Palao. The first method is by extension, or aggregation. This method implies that the extended grants follow the fortunes of the original privilege. The other method *ad instar* is twofold: first dependently on the initial privilege and similarly affected; second inde-

---

47 Schmalzgrueber, *o.c.*, lib. V, tit. XXXIII, n. 88.

48 Palao, *o.c.*, tr. 3, disp. 4, p. 2, § 9, n. 1-5.

49 Schmalzgrueber, *o.c.*, lib. V, tit. XXXIII, n. 77-79.

pendently of the first privilege so that it retains all its force without reference to the fortunes of the first privilege.

The modern way of division by communication is *in forma aeque principali,* and *forma accessoria.* Privileges of the first class are independent, those of the second are not. In this way Maroto, following the Code, joins the aggregations and extensions of Palao and Schmalzgrueber in one group, and leaves the *ad instar* privileges in a separate class.[50]

B. *Present Legislation concerning the Communication of Privileges.*

**Can. 64. Per communicationem privilegiorum, etiam in forma aeque principali, ea tantum privilegia impertita censentur, quae directe, perpetuo et sine relatione ad certum locum aut rem aut personam concessa fuerant primo privilegiario, habita etiam ratione capacitatis subiecti, cui fit communicatio.**

Canon 64 lays down the present law concerning communication of privileges even in *forma aeque principali.* Four items must be kept in mind: manner of concession, stability of the privilege, extent, and capacity.

*Directe.* A privilege is conceded directly when the beneficiary, whether a moral or physical person, is the immediate object of the Superior's good will. For instance, if an institute asks the Holy Father for the privilege of saying a proper mass in honor of some mystery or saint, the concession of this favor would be direct. In order to have the entire institute benefit by this concession, the extent of the grant must be well defined. This is no new provision, for even in the time of Urban VIII a constitution of the Pope was necessary to extend the feast of Blessed Margaret of Cortona, now

50 Maroto, *o.c.*, v. I, n. 298.

canonized, to the entire Order of Saint Francis. Until December 13, 1623, this feast was confined to the city of Cortona. The constitution *Caelestis aquae* extended the feast.[51]

Now, suppose a Congregation petitioned the Holy Father to communicate the privileges of the Franciscans to it. Should the Pope accede to the request, the privileged Congregation could then celebrate the feast of Saint Margaret. If then a second institute were granted communication of the privileges enjoyed by the Congregation just mentioned, the feast of Saint Margaret would not be communicated because the Congregation did not receive it directly.

Another case: a society is joined to an archconfraternity according to the provisions of canons 720-723. According to canon 722 only those privileges would be communicated which had been the object of direct concession by the Holy See. Should some privileges have been conceded to the archconfraternity by means of communication, the same privilege would not accrue to the aggregated society.[52]

In the same manner that communicated privileges cannot themselves be subject to further communication, so, too, privileges which arise from custom, or prescription are not subject to communication. Hence, if a society by constant use thru the prescribed number of years[53] obtains a privilege, the favor indeed is valid before the law, but it is not liable to communication. Similarly should an individual person legitimately prescribe a privilege, it is valid but it does not become the source of communication.

*Perpetuo.* This word excludes all favors granted for a limited time. Consequently all quinquennial, or decennial privileges are excluded from communication.

---

51 Bull. Rom. tom. 13, p. 80.
52 Vermeersch-Creusen, *o.c.*, v. I, n. 713.
53 Can. 27, § 1.

But in order that the concession might be permanent, it is not necessary that this precise word be found in the rescript. Barbosa mentions several of similar force: *in infinitum, semper, in saecula saeculorum,* etc.[54]

*Sine relatione.* Relatively likewise excludes communication. The reason is evident and flows from the object of the privilege. If a privilege were granted to honor the tomb of a particular saint, or a miraculous picture, no foundation would exist for the communicated privilege. Thus, the proper masses conceded to religious were not communicated.[55]

*Capacitas.* The three requisites named above considered privileges from the aspect of the grant itself. The fourth requisite, however, considers the capacity of the grantee to receive a definite privilege.

Incapacity can arise from several sources. Thus, for example, religious women are incapable of receiving privileges relative to the exercise of Sacred Orders. Again the rule of a society may forbid some activity, e. g., acquisition of property. No matter how the incapacity of the grantee exists, he cannot enjoy privileges which might be communicated to him.

Privileges communicated *in forma aeque principali* retain their full force irrespective of the possible increase, decrease, or loss of the original privileges. Religious Orders enjoyed this form of communication until the time of the New Code.[56]

---

[54] Barbosa, *o.c., Dictiones Usufrequentiores,* CCLIV, CLXIII.

[55] S. C. R., 20 Mar., 1706, Coll. n. 269.

[56] Noldin, *Theologia Moralis,* (Oeniponte, 1921), 13 ed., v. I, n. 194.

**Can. 65. Cum privilegia acquiruntur per communicationem in forma accessoria, augentur, imminuuntur, vel amittuntur ipso facto, si forte augeantur, imminuantur, vel cessent in principali privilegiario; secus si acquiruntur per communicationem in forma aeque principali.**

Assuming the four requisites outlined above for the communication of privileges, a further restriction is placed on communication *in forma accessoria. Accessorium* has reference only to the privilege. It does not consider the dignity of the person who benefits by this method of communication. It may occur that the second grantee may be even more worthy of a privilege that the first, yet nevertheless, should the first grantee lose his privilege, the second grantee would likewise lose his privilege.

The present legislation clarifies the former legislation.[57] Whatever happens to the original grant, whether it increases, or decreases, or ceases, the accessory privilege is similarly affected.[58] Privileges and indulgences accruing to aggregated societies come under this head.[59] The Sacred Congregation of Indulgences decided the question of indulgences on January 31, 1893.[60] The question was asked whether indulgences revoked by the Pope could nevertheless be enjoyed by those to whom these indulgences had been communicated, unless there were express mention of revocation. The answer was: *negative immo falsa.*

Nuns with their novices receive communicated privi-

---

57 Cf. Palao, *o.c.*, tr. 3, disp. 4, p. 2, 9, n. 1-5; Schmalzgrueber, *o.c.*, lib. V, tit. XXXIII, n. 77-79.

58 Augustine, *A Commentary on the New Code of Canon Law,* (St. Louis, 1921) 4 ed., v. I, p. 158.

59 Blat, *Commentarium in Textum Codicis Iuris Canonici,* (Romae, 1921), v. I, n. 133.

60 ASS. v. XXV, p. 508.

61 C. 613, § 2; c. 567, § 1.

leges *in forma accessoria.*[61] Their servants also are included.[62]

Religious of simple vows do not receive communication of privileges, but enjoy only those privileges which are received by formal concession.[63]

### C. *The present Value of Privileges obtained before the Code by the communication of Privileges.*

In regard to communication of privileges it must be kept in mind precisely what kind of communication is forbidden by the terms of the entire canon 613.[64] Altho it may be said that a general principle embodying total exclusion of communication of privileges among the religious is enunciated in the first paragraph of canon 613, then, obviously, an exception is made in the second paragraph of the same canon.

In the case of nuns, communication of privileges *in forma accessoria* still exists. Practically speaking, the revocation of communication of privileges among the religious is confined to communication *in forma aeque principali.*

The authors who have commented on canon 613, § 1, do not agree on the interpretation of the new law. In order to set forth clearly the matter for discussion, let us see what is admitted. All agree that as a practical rule, the first paragraph of canon 613 refers to communication of privileges *in forma aeque principali.* Then all agree that this form of communication is forbidden in the future. At this point unanimity ceases. Authors

---

62 Cocchi, *Commentarium in Codicem Iuris Canonici*, (Taurinorum Augustae, 1921), v. I, n. 117; Noldin, *o.c.*, v. I, n. 194.

63 Augustine, *o.c.*, v. III, p. 511.

64 Can. 613, § 1. *Quaelibet religio iis tantum privilegiis gaudet, quae vel hoc in Codice continentur, vel a Sede Apostolica directe eidem concessa fuerint, exclusa in posterum qualibet communicatione. 2. Privilegia quibus gaudet Ordo regularis, competunt quoque monialibus eiusdem Ordinis, quatenus eorum sint capaces.*

disagree on the present value of privileges obtained in the past by communication. The question is important and the opposing sides, at least in their practical conclusions are well defined.

Prummer,[65] for instance, argues that these privileges are still valid. His reasons are: (a) one hundred years, or immemorial possession induces the presumption that a privilege was granted; (b) all privileges not expressly revoked remain in force according to canon 4;[66] (c) the word *fuerint* in canon 613, § 1, refers to the future: this word is to be understood with *in posterum*.

Vermeersch[67] bases his argument on the requisite of canon 4. This canon demands express revocation. Vermeersch holds that privileges obtained in the past by communication are still valid because canon 613, § 1 can be interpreted in this way. At least express revocation is not evident. Besides this basic argument, Vermeersch maintains that a strict literal interpretation of the first paragraph of canon 613 would be foreign to the mind of the legislator as the Orders have enjoyed centuries of use of some of these privileges. A practical reason also influences Vermeersch. He says serious doubts would arise in regard to all privileges of religious since it would be difficult to distinguish how the privileges had been obtained. Lastly Vermeersch says that the lenient interpretation is received in Rome.

Brandys[68] argues in the same way as Vermeersch, allowing privileges communicated in the past to continue.

Fanfani[69] rests his case on canon 4. According to

---

65 Prummer, *Manuale Iuris Canonici*, (Friburgi Briscoviae, 1920), 2 ed., praenotamen ad q. 239.

66 Can. 4. *Iura aliis quaesita, itemque privilegia atque indulta quae, ab Apostolica Sede ad haec usque tempora personis sive physicis sive moralibus concessa, in usu adhuc sunt nec revocata, integra manent, nisi huius Codicis canonibus expresse revocentur.*

67 Vermeersch-Creusen, *o.c.*, v. I, n. 615.

68 Brandys, *Kirchliches Rechtsbuch*, (Paderborn, 1920), 2 ed., n. 89.

69 Fanfani, *De Iure Religiosorum*, (Taurini-Romae, 1925), 2 ed., p. 362.

Fanfani, the question cannot be solved from the wording of canon 613, § 1. Consequently canon 4 is to be applied. Finally, *in dubiis melior est conditio possidentis.*

Papi,[70] Woywod,[71] and Schaefer[72] bring no new argument. They satisfy themselves by comparing canons 4 and 613, § 1.

Augustine[73] states that the law in question is not retroactive, and hence the Orders may retain what they possess except where the Code rules otherwise.

Larraona, in the periodical *Commentarium pro Religiosis*[74] inclines to the same lenient interpretation of the new law on the communication of privileges among the religious.

On the other hand Blat[75] takes sharp issue with the contentions of the above authors. The word *tantum* decides the issue. This expression has a taxative meaning. It includes only the items mentioned. Everything else is excluded. Blat cites Barbosa for the juridical force of the word *tantum.* Now, according to canon 613, § 1, each religion (*quaelibet religio*) enjoys only those privileges contained in the Code, or directly conceded by the Holy See. All communication, then, according to this paragraph, is excluded for religious. The clause *exclusa in posterum qualibet communicatione* is to be taken with the word *tantum.* Hence even communication *in forma accessoria* is eliminated in principle. This form, however, is immediately conceded to nuns relative to privilege existing in the same Order.

Fuhrich is just as emphatic for the clause *iis tantum privilegiis gaudet.*[76] Of the same opinion are Chelodi,[77]

70 Papi, *Religious in Church Law,* (New York, 1924), p. 263.
71 Woywod, *A Practical Commentary on the Code of Canon Law,* (New York, 1925), v. I, n. 48, 529.
72 Schaefer, *Das Ordensrecht,* (Munster, 1923), p. 271.
73 Augustine, *o.c.,* v. III, p. 333-4.
74 *Commentarium pro Religiosis,* v. III, p. 205-214.
75 Blat, *o.c.,* v. II, n. 689.
76 Fuhrich, *De Religiosis,* (Oeniponte, 1919), n. 145.
77 Chelodi, *Ius de Personis,* (Tridenti, 1922), n. 280.

Leitner,[78] Cicognani,[79] Egger,[80] and *Il Monitore Ecclesiastico.*[81]

Which is the correct interpretation of canon 613, § 1? An analysis of the wording of the canon seems to favor the same conclusion which Blat proposes. Before the Code communication was recognized as a legitimate source of privilege. In the present legislation for religious it is not numbered among the only two sources recognized. Hence at least from its positive exclusion, communication of privileges for religious must be regarded as revoked. The present tense of the verb *gaudet* means that any privilege not valid at the time of the Code is abolished.

The arguments contrary to this opinion can practically be reduced to five: (1) the alleged omission to revoke expressly; (2) Possession of one hundred years induces the presumption that a privilege was granted; (3) Revocation of communicated privileges would be foreign to the mind of the legislator; (4) The law of canon 613, § 1 is not retroactive; (5) The verb *concessa fuerint* is future time.

These arguments do not seem to be convincing. But in order that due consideration may be accorded them, each one will be examined separately.

(1) Canon 4 demands express revocation in order that a privilege contrary to the present law may cease. It does not, however, determine what formula, if any, must be used. Express revocation means explicit revocation. This can be had either by the use of the customary formula *revocato privilegio,*[82] or by the positive exclusion of an item when, to obtain force, it would have

78 *Leitner, Handbuch des katholischen Kirchenrechts,* (Regensburg, 1922), 2 ed. v. III, § 3, n. 8, 1, 2.

79 Cicognani, *o.c.,* p. 279.

80 Egger, *Das neue Ordensrecht,* (Freiburg, 1919), p. 23.

81 *Il Monitore Ecclesiastico,* anno 1918, p. 194, 366-7.

82 E.g., 519; 522; 1576, § 1.

to be mentioned.[83] Obviously, the usual formula given above is not employed in canon 613, § 1. But explicit revocation is obtained by the positive exclusion of communication as a source of privilege.[84] The use of the present tense (*gaudet*) specifies the time when the privileges of religious are valid.[85] When three methods of obtaining privileges are possible and only two are allowed, it follows that the third is forbidden. For this reason it seems that canon 4 gives small comfort towards retaining such privileges. Privileges obtained in the past thru communication seem to be revoked by the clause *vel a Sede Apostolica directe eidem concessa fuerint.* Communicated privileges were never *directly* obtained from the Holy See.

(2) Canon 63, § 2 gives the rule for presumed privileges. A presumption is a probable conjecture of something uncertain. It is called an improper proof.[86] When the truth is known, the presumption yields to it. No matter how long the presumption may last, it is always subject to this reversal. Its nature does not change. Granting, for a moment, that communicated privileges can be considered as presumed privileges, their status would not be the same as privileges obtained by concession. Therefore, if a decision be made, such as is found in canon 613, § 1, it is evident that the presumption is destroyed, and with it the privilege presumed to have been granted. But the assumption that communicated privileges can be presumed as conceded privileges is not true. The privileges obtained thru communication were not used with the intention of introducing a custom, but on the contrary, were used as privileges directly conceded to others.[87]

---

83 E.g., Necessary quasi-domicile is excluded by canon 93.
84 Chelodi, *o.c.*, n. 280.
85 Leitner, *o.c.*, l.c.
86 Noval, *De Iudiciis*, (Augustae Taurinorum, 1920), n. 559.
87 Fuhrich, *o.c.*, n. 145.

(3) When an argument deals with what may be foreign to the mind of the legislator, frequently no sure or decisive matter is at hand. Reasons of convenience will always be present, and for both sides of a question. What may appear proper to one will seem improper to another. At any rate, nothing more could be obtained from such an argument than a reason similar to *epikeia,* which interpretation always supposes the law to exist, and to consult the majority of cases. However, *epekeia* is inadmissible here because of the definite legislation. Granted, as Vermeersch says, that the new legislation would deprive the Orders of privileges used for centuries:[88] this would not affect a positive law evidently made to limit the number of privileges. A precedent is found in the Bull of Pius IV, *In principis,* which revoked all privileges contrary to the decrees of the Council of Trent.[89] This Council ushered in a new epoch. To further the common observance of its decrees, privileges contrary to the decrees were revoked. The present Code begins a new canonical epoch, and the same reason holds today as for centuries ago. The common law is to be observed unless legitimate exceptions are made.

(4) Retroactivity of laws is not presumed.[90] The common good demands that rights acquired in the past be left undisturbed unless some special reason decree otherwise.[91] Augustine's argument from the non-retroactive force of the law in canon 613, § 1 would be valid if there would be a possibility of considering retroactivity in connection with this canon. But Augustine misapplies the notion of retroactivity. There is no question of retroactivity, or non-retroactivity in canon 613, § 1. The validity of acts performed in the past by reason of communicated privileges is not touched at all by the legis-

88 Vermeersch-Creusen, *o.c.*, v. I, n. 615.
89 Conc. Trident. Bulla S.D.N.D.Pii Papae quarti, February 24, 1565.
90 Can. 10.
91 Vermeersch-Creusen, *o.c.*, v. I, n. 44.

lation of the New Code. The present right is removed by canon 613, § 1. This follows from the exclusion of communication as a source of privilege for religious.

(5) The argument from the tense and mood of the verb *concessa fuerint* offers some difficulty. If this is the perfect subjunctive form, implying potentiality[92] a doubt can arise concerning the revocation of privileges communicated before the Code. But it seems that this idea of potentiality can hardly exist with the collocation of words in the last clause of the paragraph *exclusa in posterum qualibet communicatione.* This clause taken with the present tense of the principal verb *gaudet* eliminates all manner of communication. In the very next paragraph the Code makes an exception to the rule. In order to have the last clause of the first paragraph construed with the possibly potential meaning of *concessa fuerint,* it would have to read *exclusa qualibet in posterum communicatione.*[93]

The authorized English version of the canons concerning religious leaves little doubt that potentiality is not the implication of *concessa fuerint.*[94] While this English translation has not the force of law, it does afford a confirmatory argument for the strict interpretation of the canon in question. Canon 613, § 1 reads: *East Institute enjoys those privileges only which are contained in the Code, or may have been directly conceded to it by the Apostolic See; every communication of privileges is henceforth excluded.*

In conclusion, altho the wording of canon 613, § 1 seems to exclude a lenient interpretation, yet something must be said for the extrinsic authority of the authors who hold this opinion. The list of authors arrayed on the side of the lenient opinion is not insignificant, and

---

92 *Commentarium pro Religiosis,* v. III, p. 212.
93 Chelodi, *o.c.,* n. 280, p. 438, ft. 1.
94 *Canonical Legislation concerning Religious; authorized English Translation,* (Rome, 1919).

it would be too much to maintain that no extrinsic authority at all attaches to their opinion. Hence an authoritative interpretation of this canon by the Pontifical Commission will be welcomed. Meanwhile, in practice, the reliable *Monitore Ecclesiastico* says: We know that the application of canon 613 is suspended until the Sacred Congregation for Religious finishes its work of revising the privileges of the various religious Institutes.[95] The reliability of the *Monitore Ecclesiastico* cannot be gainsaid. Yet it is not beyond a legitimate desire to wish that the source of this information had been made public.

### 3. *Custom as a Source of Privilege.*

The Code recognizes custom as a source of privilege. Considered in its formal aspect, custom may be defined with Bouix as *Ius per similium alicuius communitatis actuum frequentiam acquisitum*;[96] or with Wernz as *ius quod ex facto sive frequentia illa operandi resultat.*[97] The tacit consent of the legislator is sufficient to obtain a right thru custom. Hence every custom which has the express disapproval of the legislator cannot continue to exist to engender rights.[98] The Code specifies e. g., rubrics, profession of faith as some of the canons under which customs are expressly disapproved.[99] Customs which exist contrary to these prescriptions have no force whatever.

Custom itself is twofold: (a) the frequency of similar acts; (b) the right which results from this repetition.[100] The former is the material cause of the latter. The

95 *Il Monitore Ecclesiastico,* anno 1918, p. 366, ft.

96 Bouix, *De Principiis Iuris Canonici,* (Parisiis, 1882), p. 351.

97 Wernz, *o.c.,* v. I, n. 187.

98 Barbosa, *o.c., Tractatus locorum communium argumentorum iuris,* n. XXV.

99 E. g., cc. 343, § 2; 346; 396; 403; 409, § 2; 418, § 1; 455, § 1; 460, § 2; 774, § 1; 818; 978, § 3; 1006, § 5; 1041, 1056, 1181; 1356, § 1; 1408; 1492; 1525; 1576, § 1.

100 Bouix, *o.c.,* p. 350-1.

activity on the part of the community must be free, else no custom, no matter how long it exists, can be valid.

In the formation of Roman Law customs or *mores* were of prime importance. Divorce, for example, was restricted by custom and gradually some of these customs became incorporated in the written law.[101]

Justinian[102] gives the foundation for the definition of custom. He says: *sine scripto ius venit quod usus approbavit, nam diuturni mores consensu utentium comprobati, leges imitantur.* In this statement the material and formal elements of custom are brought together. From this citation it seems to be evident that Justinian admitted the force of custom but some doubt is thrown on the value of the citation by a constitution of Constantine. This reads: *consuetudines ususque longaevi non vilis auctoritatis est: verum non usque adeo sui valituri momento ut rationem vincat aut legem.*[103] Ferrini after showing the relative importance of custom, reconciles these two texts by saying that Constantine's constitution referred to customs existing before laws which rearranged the matter in question.[104] Ferrini believes that another section of Justinian law represents a points of the same Constantinian law.[105] If so, the matter becomes clear, for the constitution was given even in regard to those who claimed immunity from certain public duties.

Gratian defined custom thus: *ius quoddam moribus institutum quod pro lege suscipitur cum deficit lex.*[106] Prummer[107] thinks this definition is solid because a law can be deficient in clarity, in extension, or in utility.

---

101 Bonfante, *Storia di Diritto Romano*, p. 215, 291.
102 I, 1, 2, 9.
103 In Maroto, *o.c.*, n. 251.
104 Ferrini, *Pandetti*, n. 17.
105 C. 1, 11, 65, (64).
106 C. 5, D. I.
107 Prummer, *Manuale Theologiae Moralis*, (Friburgi Briscoviae, 1923), v. I, n. 272.

DeAngelis[108] is not so kind to Gratian's definition because it seems to apply only to customs beyond the law, with a possibility of extending the definition to customs contrary to the law. But it certainly does not allow for customs according to the law.

In one place Gratian denies the validity of a particular custom contrary to the law,[109] and in another place admits that a custom can abrogate laws and canons.[110] Alexander III acknowledged the force of custom,[111] and Gregory IX canonized the doctrine that a custom can abrogate a law.[112]

The question of custom is not an easy one. In the universal Church much more certitude concerning the value of a custom can be obtained than in a particular diocese or church. At times it will be difficult to determine whether or not a custom has any value. In such a predicament Cardenas[113] lays down two rules which should give some assurance either in favor of the custom, or against it. Cardenas says: (1) if all the people in a diocese are morally certain that a custom originated from a legitimate cause, the custom has legal value. Tradition of the custom could have been handed to succeeding generations until the original time of introduction would be forgotten. The consensus of practically all the people is full proof. (2) If this universal belief is not present, the custom is doubtful since full proof in testimony of a fact cannot be had. However, if the dissenting portion of the community is negligible, or un-

108 De Angelis, *Praelectiones Iuris Canonici*, (Romae, 1877), lib. I, tit. IV, n. 1.

109 C. 4, D.XI, dictum: *Cum vero nec sacris canonibus, nec humanis legibus consuetudo obviare monstratur, inconcussa servanda est.*

110 C. 3, D.IV, dictum: *Sicut enim moribus utentium in contrarium nonnullae leges hodie abrogatae sunt, ita moribus utentium ipsae leges confirmantur.*

111 C. 8, X, *de sententia et re iudicata*, II, 27.

112 C. 11, X, *de consuetudine*, I, 4; Vecchiotti, *o.c.*, lib. I, c. II, § 27.

113 Cardenas, *Crisis Theologica*, (Venetiis, 1700), disp. XXIII, c. V, art. 13-14.

worthy of belief, it can be brushed aside and the custom considered legitimate.

Particular legislation concerning a privilege introduced by custom, will at times be a delicate matter. For example, should a custom contrary to the general law of the Church exist in a diocese it may be difficult, if not impossible to eradicate it. In such a situation a Bishop would far exceed his rights if he made a synodal law recognizing this custom. Mansi uses strong language in describing such a departure from the constituted order of procedure: *nimia esset arrogantia, si Episcopus legem conderet contra legem Superioris.*[114]

Still it cannot be denied that customs contrary to the general law did exist and were difficult to remove. Benedict XIV[115] praises the prudence of Saint Charles Borromeo when the latter found himself in such a difficult position. In Milan a custom existed in regard to alienation of ecclesiastical property. This custom was contrary to the Apostolic constitutions. Saint Charles refused to legislate in this matter, but instead consulted Rome about the best course to pursue. An answer was given to Saint Charles that the custom could not remain in force and that the general law of the Church was to be followed.

On the other hand Benedict XIV[116] warns against a hasty synodal law with a view towards eradicating a custom. Such action might lead to endless opposition to the detriment of souls. The prudent way would be to explain the case fully to the Holy See and abide by its wise disposition.

Custom can be divided thus[117]: (a) in respect of extent, customs are *universal, general,* or *special* according

114 Mansi, *Epitome Iuris Canonici,* (Mechliniae, 1824), verb. consuetudo.

115 Benedict XIV, *De Synodo Diocesana,* (Romae, 1806), lib. IX, c. VIII, n. 9; lib. XII, c. VIII, n. 10.

116 Benedict XIV, *o.c.,* lib. XI, c. V, n. 1.

117 Maroto, *o.c.,* v. I, n. 250; Bouix, *o.c.,* p. 352.

as the custom exists in the universal Church, a province or diocese, or in a society; (b) in respect of the law itself, customs are *according, contrary,* or *beyond the law*; (c) in respect of the manner of usage, customs are *judicial,* or *extra judicial* according as the customs have their proper place in trials or outside of them; (d) in respect of time, customs are *ordinary, centennial,* or *immemorial* according as the custom is of forty years duration, one hundred years, or the time of origin forgotten.

Only customs contrary to the law, and beyond it are of any importance in regard to privileges. Canon 25 says that the competent Superior is the only one who can give legal force to a custom. Thus Canon Law differs from Roman Law because subjects in ecclesiastical law have no part in making laws.[118] The Historical School, *e. g.,* Shulte, Sohm, etc., attempted to apply the principles of Roman Law to Canon Law, but as Wernz[119] points out they contradicted the teaching of the Church.[120] All jurisdiction resides in the Pope, and thru him in the Bishops: the faithful have no legislative power.[121]

Tacit consent of the competent Superior suffices for the validity of a custom, but even legal consent such as is given in canons 27 and 28 is enough to make the custom legitimate. This was already admitted in the Decretals of Gregory IX.[122]

The matter, or substance of the custom must be reasonable.[123] Therefore no custom, and thru it a privilege, can be introduced contrary to natural, or divine law,[124] or which is expressly declared to be unreasonable. In

---

118 Maroto, *o.c.,* v. I, n. 252.
119 Wernz, *o.c.,* v. I, n. 188.
120 C. 3, X, *de consuetudine,* I, 4.
121 Bellarminus, *o.c.,* lib. IV, c. XV; Bouquillon, *o.c.,* n. 96.
122 C. 11, X, *de consuetudine,* I, 4.
123 Maroto, *o.c.,* v. I, n. 252.
124 C. 27, § 1; C. 10, 11, X, *de consuetudine,* I, 4; c. 30, X, *de praebendis et dignitatibus,* III, 5; Bouix, *o.c.,* p. 364.

the Code every custom which is expressly reprobated is unreasonable.[125]

Superiors are the judges of the reasonableness of a custom. In case of doubt, possession will argue in favor of the custom.[126]

The time required by the Code for the concession of privilege thru custom is determined according to the respective law in the matter. Customs contrary to ordinary laws become legal after forty continuous and complete years. Customs, however, contrary to a law which contains a clause prohibiting customs do not become legitimate until one hundred years are completed. Immemorial customs likewise cause prejudice to the last-named laws.[127]

### 4. *Prescription as a Source of Privilege.*

Prescription is defined: *Modus legitimus acquirendi ius vel liberationem aliquam procedens per possessionem modo et tempore a legibus continuatam.*[128] Primarily, prescription is one of the legal exceptions by which good faith coupled with legitimate and continued possession supersede the rights of a preceding owner. Prescription has its foundation in human law, and not in natural law. The latter would recognize an abandoned right as always belonging to the owner, while the former legally dispossesses the owner and transfers the right to another. Prescription is justified by the elimination of the confusion which would result from years of unknown ownership.

Prescription is divided into *formal and causal.* Formal prescription is the right acquired after the requirements of the law have been fulfilled. Causal prescrip-

---

125 Can. 27, § 2.
126 De Angelis, *o.c.*, lib. I, tit. IV, n. 6.
127 Can. 27, § 1.
128 Santi, *Praelectiones Iuris Canonici*, (Ratisbonae, 1886), lib. II, tit. XXVI, n. 1.

tion consists in the actions which tend toward obtaining formal prescription.[129]

The qualities necessary for valid prescription must be considered carefully. In the first place it is essential to know that not every thing is subject to prescription. Canon 1509[130] names items that are not liable to prescription. For example, the privilege of exemption from all visitation can never be prescribed. Similarly, the exemption accorded religious Orders cannot be prescribed by a Congregation because the only source of this privilege is Apostolic concession. Good faith is necessary according to the Rule of Law *possessor malae fide ullo tempore non praescribit.*[131] A just title is necessary. By this it is understood that transferable dominion exists. Possession is absolutely essential to prescription, for without it prescription is unintelligible.[132]

Prescription is properly understood in acquiring rights which, according to the common law, would belong to another. Thus such jurisdiction which has its sole source in ecclesiastical law can be prescribed by a cleric.[133] Similarly, the jurisdiction of an Archbishop, or Bishop can be prescribed by a Patriarch. Such a case was decided by Innocent III in his letter to the Archbishop of Turo.[134] Again Innocent III decided in favor of a prescription in the case of delinquent clerics. The

---

129 Santi, *o.c.*, l.c., n. 4.

130 Can. 1509. *Praescriptioni obnoxia non sunt: 1. Quae sunt iuris divini sive naturalis sive positivi; 2. Quae obtineri possunt ex solo privilegio apostolico; 3. Iura spiritualia, quorum laici non sunt capaces, si agatur de praescriptione in commodum laicorum; 4. Fines certi et indubii provinciarum ecclesiasticarum dioecesium, paroeciarum, vicariatuum apostolicorum, praefecturarum apostolicarum, abbatiarum vel praelaturarum nullius; 5. Eleemosynae et onera Missarum; 6. Beneficium ecclesiasticum sine titulo; 7. Ius visitationis et obedientiae, ita ut subditi a nullo Praelato visitari possint et nulli Praelato iam subsint; 8. Solutio cathedratici.*

131 R.J. 2 in VI.

132 R.J. 3 in VI.

133 Jurisdiction received from divine law is not subject to prescription: can. 1509, n. 1.

134 C. 9, X, *de officio iudicis ordinarii*, I, 31.

Pope writes that Bishops are to judge their subjects unless a custom or privilege rule otherwise.[135]

The time required to prescribe a privilege against the rights of the Holy See is one hundred years.[136] This doctrine was already taught by Gratian: *Venerandae Romanae leges, divinitus per ora principum promulgatae, reum eius prescriptionem non nisi per centum annos admittunt.*[137] Innocent III took up the same principle,[138] and Boniface VIII made a similar ruling.[139]

Thirty years are sufficient to prescribe against the rights of a moral person inferior to the Holy See.[140]

Prescription of the rights of a Bishop, and indeed of any physical person, is not included in canon 1511. Another canon (1508) says that the respective law of the nation is to be followed. Should no law be found to cover the case, refuge will have to be taken in the law made for similar cases.[141] Perhaps thirty years would suffice for prescription against the rights of a Bishop. Vermeersch holds this opinion.[142] But this interpretation does not agree with another canon.[143] While it is true that custom and prescription are not the same, still the latter is a kind of private custom. An individual person cannot induce a custom, but he can prescribe.[144] Now in canon 27, § 1, it is stated that a period of forty years is necessary to act legally against an ecclesiastical law. Jurisdiction of Bishops come under this head. Therefore it seems that forty, and not thirty years are

---

135 C. 13, X, *de foro competenti*, II, 2.
136 Can. 1511, § 1.
137 C. 17, C, XVI, q. 3.
138 C. 13, 14 X, *de praescriptionibus*, II, 26; c. 4, X, *de confirmatione utili vel inutili*, II, 30.
139 C. 2, *de praescriptionibus*, II, 13 in VI.
140 Can. 1511, § 2.
141 Can. 20.
142 Vermeersch-Creusen, *o.c.*, v. I, n. 130.
143 Can. 27, § 1.
144 Cicognani, *o.c.*, p. 282.

necessary for prescription.[145] Besides a Bishop is not considered a moral person in regard to his personal jurisdiction, but only in relation to the rights of his diocese which he embodies in his only own person. Hence it seems to be incorrect to apply prescription against moral persons to prescription against individual rights of a Prelate.

### 5. *Presumption of Privileges.*

**Can. 63, § 2. Possessio centenaria vel immemorabilis inducit praesumptionem concessi privilegii.**

Presumption is defined in canon 1825, § 1. *Praesumptio est rei incertae probabilis coniectura.* The same canon divides presumptions into *praesumptiones iuris,* and *praesumptiones hominis.* The former are determined by law: the latter are formed by a judge. *Praesumptio iuris* is further divided into *praesumptio iuris simpliciter,* and *praesumptio iuris et de iure.*

The value of the several classes varies. Legal presumptions carry great weight, and must be accepted by all within the proper sphere of their content, and according to the probative force assigned to them by law. Thus *praesumptio iuris simpliciter* furnishes a basis for forming a judgment but it admits both direct and indirect contrary proof: *praesumptio iuris et de iure* cannot be attacked directly but is assailable only in so far as its foundation may be destroyed.[146] Both of these presumptions have objective force in law. A judge is not free to admit or reject them. Thus the testimony of two or more witnesses, with all the qualifications demanded in canon 1791, § 2 must be accepted as sufficient proof.[147]

*Praesumptio hominis* will have an indefinite value according to the reasons proposed by each judge. This

---

145 Cocchi, *o.c.*, v. I, n. 117.
146 Can. 1826.
147 Noval, *o.c.*, n. 512.

value is entirely personal and may mean nothing at all to another judge. Thus a judge *secundae instantiae* may reject all the presumptions of the court from which the appellation came.

The legal foundation for the value of presumption, at least in regard to privileges, is based on the tolerance of the legislator. Benedict XIV takes occasion to examine this point in discussing the administration of the Sacrament of Confirmation by Greek priests. The eminent canonist writes that the administration of the Sacrament of Confirmation by Greek priests is not expressly condemned and therefore it is to be considered valid *ob tacitam saltem privilegium a Sede Apostolica illis concessum: cuius quidem privilegii praesumptionem inducit ipsamet conniventia, et tolerantia Romanorum Pontificum, qui praedictum Graecorum morem scientes non contradixerunt, nec unquam illum damnarunt.*[148]

The probative force of a presumption relative to a privilege was admitted by Pope Nicholas I in his letter to the Archbishop of Bourges. The Pope writes that no Prelate has a right to arrogate another's jurisdiction, but that custom can change some of the canons giving rise to privileges.[149]

Innocent III likewise admitted the force of presumption in another dispute concerning alleged usurpation of jurisdiction by means of custom and prescription.[150] Alexander III similarly allowed presumption in the matter of tithes.[151]

A presumption that a privilege has been conceded relieves the grantee of the burden of proof. Mere denial of the privilege cannot be sustained, but the presumption itself can be dissolved if it should be proved that in point of fact the disputed privilege had not been conceded.

---

148 Benedict, XIV, *o.c.*, lib. VII, c. IX, n. 3.
149 C. 8, C. IX, q. 3.
150 C. 13, X, *de foro competenti*, II, 2; c. 18, X, *de praescriptionibus*, II, 26.
151 C. 4, X, *de praescriptionibus*, II, 26.

The possession essential to presumption must be real. Consequently, something held in trust cannot give rise to presumption. The object in possession may be something material concerning which a privilege can be granted, or something spiritual such as a right, or a benefice.

## CHAPTER V

## INTERPRETATION OF A PRIVILEGE.

An *interpretation* of a privilege is the explanation of the terms of a privilege. It supposes a doubt concerning the terms of the favor granted. Strictly speaking, *declaration* is not the same as interpretation for the former merely states what is contained in the grant and does not suppose it to be anything but clear. Yet the non-restrictive and non-extensive interpretation demanded in a privilege[1] can be called declarative interpretation.

Interpretation can be divided in several ways. In respect of its application, it is *extensive,* or *comprehensive.* An *extensive* interpretation enjoys great importance in matters of law. In order to have extensive interpretation, it is necessary not only to go beyond the actual verbal meaning of the law, but also to depart from the mind of the legislator.[2] However, such interpretation must not be contrary to the mind of the legislator. Reasons similar to the ones supporting a law allow for its extension to cases not included in the law itself. Innocent III thus explains his right to transfer Bishops-elect.[3]

In interpreting privileges *extensive* interpretation is of no value. A privilege concedes a special faculty. It is an extraordinary provision and consequently cannot be used as an example. Pope Alexander III wrote: *Temerarium est et indignum, aliquem sibi sua auctoritate praesumere, quod Romana ecclesia alicui, certa ra-*

1 Can. 67.

2 Reiffenstuel, *o.c.,* lib. V, tit. XXXIII, n. 93; Ferraris, *o.c.,* v. privilegium, art. 2, n. 20.

3 C. 2, X, *de translatione Episcopi,* I, 7.

*tione inspecta, singularibus voluit beneficiis indulgere.*[4] Boniface VIII sponsored identical legislation.[5]

However this does not hold for extension to possible consequences of a privilege.[6] For example, if a chapel is built within the confines of a parish and enjoys the privilege of having mass celebrated there, voluntary offerings can be accepted in that chapel. This might be considered more in the nature of comprehension than extension.

*Comprehensive* interpretation is admissible in privileges. Such an interpretation conforms to the mind of the legislator rather than to his words.[7] *Certe noverit ille, qui intentionem et voluntatem alterius variis verbis explicat, quia non debet aliquis verba considerare, sed voluntatem et intentionem, quia non debet intentio verbis deservire, sed verba intentioni.*[8] Gratian in his commentary to this canon reduces the text to an axiom: *Intentio non debet deservire verbis, sed verba intentioni.*[9] Thus, by means of comprehensive interpretation, a privilege conceded to a hospital includes those who work there, or, a privilege to say mass during an interdict includes the server, etc.

In respect of the source of the interpretation, it is *authentic, usual,* or *doctrinal.* The first is obtained by express declaration of the *Superior* who conceded the privilege. The second is had thru *custom.* The third secures its force from the *opinions of authors.*[10] The immediate and practical value of a *doctrinal* interpretation depends upon the reasons adduced by each author.

---

4 C. 9, X, *de privilegiis et excessibus privilegiatorum,* V, 33; cf. c. 8, 16, 17, 18.

5 R. J. 28 in VI: *Quae a iure communi exorbitant, nequaquam ad consequentiam sunt trahenda;* R. J. 74: *Quod alicui gratiose conceditur, trahi non debet ab aliis in exemplum.*

6 Tuschus, *o.c.,* v. VI, lit. P, concl. 734, n. 1.

7 Ferraris, *o.c.,* art. c., n. 21.

8 C. 11, C. XXII, q. 5.

9 *Dictum Gratianum.*

10 Ferraris, *o.c.,* art. c., n. 22.

An interpretation may also be *strict*, or *broad*. In no case can the words of the document be restricted to less than the meaning of the words allow, nor extend beyond the natural and juridical sense of the words. Both strict and broad interpretation have as their sole sources custom and the opinion of authors.

**Canon 67. Privilegium ex ipsius tenore aestimandum est, nec licet illud extendere aut restringere.**

**Canon 68. In dubio privilegia interpretanda sunt ad normam can. 50; sed ea semper adhibenda interpretatio, ut privilegio aucti aliquam ex indulgentia concedentis videantur gratiam consecuti.**

**Canon 70. Privilegium, nisi aliud constet, censendum est perpetuum.**

Before entering upon the discussion of the rules which must guide the interpretation of a privilege, it is well to lay down a principle which is anterior to all norms in this matter. This principle concerns the competence of interpreters. In the first place the legislator, who is alone capable of giving an authentic interpretation of a privilege, is the most competent to interpret. His will is the cause of the privilege and he is the best judge of his own benevolent intentions.[11] Innocent III, in writing to the doctors of Bologna summarizes in one short sentence the absolute competence of the legislator. He writes: *Unde ius prodiit, interpretatio quoque procedat.*[12] In regard to Apostolic privileges, Pope Innocent III is even more explicit: *cum super privilegiis sedis Apostolicae causa vertatur, nolumus de ipsis per alios iudicari.*[13] The successor of the actual legislator is

[11] Herincx, *o.c.*, disp. 4, q. 7, n. 87; Tuschus, *o.c.*, v. VI, lit. P, concl. 737, n. 1-2; Fagnanus, *o.c.*, *De verborum significatione*, c. *olim*, n. 34; De Meester, *o.c.*, n. 307.

[12] C. 31, X, *de sententia excommunicationis*, V, 39.

[13] C. 12, X, *de iudiciis*, II, 1.

equally competent to give an authentic interpretation of a privilege. *Is qui in ius succedit alterius, eo iure, quo ille uti debebit.*[14]

After the legislator himself, or his successor, those who are learned in the law are the best interpreters. But their interpretation is merely doctrinal, and depends, as has already been observed, on the reasons proposed. Extrinsic authority is likewise of some weight and, generally speaking, the judgment of Superiors can be followed in interpreting a privilege. Thus regulars can follow the interpretation of their Prelates with a safe conscience.[15]

Obviously, when a privilege is entirely free from ambiguity it needs no interpretation. The purpose of interpretation is to discover what the legislator intends to concede, and hence, interpretation could have no place in a privilege which is itself sufficiently clear. A re-examination of the document containing a privilege may be necessary in order to find the exact intentions of the legislator. Thus the Decretals contain the remarks of Alexander III in reference to the many privileges of the Templars: *totum ex inspectione privilegiorum suorum, plenius advertere potes, et secundum quod inveneris, ita observes.*[16] The same Pontiff writes to one of his legates: *Inspicienda sunt ergo ipsarum ecclesiarum privilegia, et ipsorum tenor est diligentius attendendus.*[17]

As a corollary from these texts it follows that both *extension* and *restriction* are forbidden. *Extension*, as noted above, is entirely without application in privileges. This is so true that a person with an even better reason for enjoying a privilege would nevertheless not possess it without specific concession.[18] The reason is that all

---

14 R.J. 46 in VI.
15 Herincx, *o.c.*, l.c.
16 C. 7, X, *de privilegiis et excessibus privilegiatorum*, V. 33.
17 C. 8, X, *de privilegiis et excessibus privilegiatorum*, V. 33.
18 Herincx, *o.c.*, disp. 4, q. 7, n. 91; Palao, *o.c.*, tr. 3, disp. 4, p. 13, n. 1; Amort, *o.c.*, lib. V, tit. XXXIII, n. 16; Sanguineti, *o.c.*, n. 139.

the power and efficacy of a privilege come from the will of the competent Superior.[19] Alexander III thus decided the matter in respect of exemption from tithes: *licet de benignitate sedis apostolicae sit vobis indultum, ut de laboribus vestris, quos propriis manibus vel sumptibus colitis, nemini decimas solvere teneamini; propter hoc tamen non est licitum vobis cuilibet decimas de terris vestris subtrahere, quas aliis traditis excolendas.*[20] Innocent III gave a similar decision in regard to exemption from possible penalties. The canons attached to the chapel of the Duke of Burgundy enjoyed the privilege that no Archbishop or Bishop could fulminate a decree of excommunication, interdict, or suspension against any one of their number. This privilege was a local and personal one. The canons enjoyed exemption from penalties not in their own right entirely, but by reason of their service in the ducal chapter. Nevertheless, some of the canons who rendered service in parish churches refused to submit to penal sentences inflicted because of crimes commited whilè in such parish service. Upon the Bishop's appeal to Rome, the Pope replied: *Quocirca fraternitati presentium auctoritate mandamus, quatenus, in quantum exempti sunt eiusdem ratione capellae, apostolicis privilegiis deferas reverenter; sed, in quantum ratione parochialium ecclesiarum vel alias iurisdictionem tuam respicere dignoscuntur, officii tui debitum in eosdem libere prosequaris.*[21] The Council of Trent cited this letter and confirmed it.[22] Similar extensive interpretations were rejected by Innocent III in his letter to the Bishops of Auson and Elide,[23] and again in the general council held during his reign.[24] Boniface VIII found it necessary to lay down the exact extent of exemption

19 Ballerini, *o.c.*, v. I, n. 391, I.
20 C. 11, X, *de decimis, primitiis et oblationibus*, III, 30.
21 C. 16, *de privilegiis et excessibus privilegiatorum*, V, 33 in VI.
22 Sess. XXIV *de reformatione*, c. 11.
23 C. 18, 19, X, *de privilegiis et excessibus privilegiatorum*, V, 33.
24 C. 24, X, *de privilegiis et excessibus privilegiatorum*, V, 33.

so that it would not be so flexible as to nullify all jurisdiction of the Bishop.[25]

Benedict XIV, in his constitution *Apostolica Indulta*, August 5, 1744, calls attention to the abuses arising from the free interpretation of the *Bulla Cruciatae*.[26] He says that these abuses are foreign to the mind and the will of the Pontiffs who made the concessions. Accordingly, he finds it necessary to make precise regulations covering the provisions of this already ample privilege. The Sacred Congregation of Rites was obliged to give similar decrees. For instance, a feast celebrated in Spain could not be extended to Portugal.[27] Again the privilege of celebrating certain feasts conceded to the Archdiocese of Cincinnati could not be extended to other dioceses altho they used the same Ordo.[28]

Pope Pius X adhered to the same principle in his *motu proprio* of February 21, 1905. This *motu proprio, Inter multiplices,* defined the privileges of the *Protonotarii,* and precisely set the limits of place, time, and function in which these privileges could be used.[29]

*Restriction* of a privilege is also forbidden. This prohibition does not, ordinarily, refer to the grantee. Since the entire use of at least strict privileges[30] is left to the grantee, he can use all the privilege, or only a part as he sees fit. Everyone else, however, is obliged to allow full use of the privilege, and cannot curtail the legitimate use of the privilege in any way. Indirect restriction is also forbidden, for the reason that while preserving the letter of the privilege, it actually limits the free use of the grant. Honorius III expressly forbade this indirect restriction of a privilege.[31]

25 C. 9, *de privilegiis et excessibus privilegiatorum,* V. 33 in VI.
26 Fontes, v. I, n. 344.
27 Dec. Auth. S.R.C., n. 179 ad 3.
28 Coll. n. 1592.
29 Dec. Auth. S.R.C., n. 4154, n. 80.
30 As distinct from privileges accorded a state, or a community.
31 C. 26, X, *de privilegiis et excessibus privilegiatorum,* V, 33.

*Rules governing the interpretation of privileges.*

FUNDAMENTAL RULE. The fundamental rule for the interpretation of privileges can scarcely be better expressed than in the way it is found in the Code: *Ea semper adhibenda interpretatio, ut privilegio aucti aliquam ex indulgentia concedentis videantur gratiam consecuti.*[32] If the essence of a privilege consists in the concession of a favor not possible of attainment under the law, then, every interpretation must preserve this element inviolate.[33] A privilege would be useless if it were hedged in with so many formalities that it would result in something attainable in law. For instance, if a priest obtains the privilege to celebrate mass on a portable altar, his privilege must mean *per modum habitus.* It cannot mean for a few occasions, e. g., as long as possible infirmity may last, because he would not need a privilege for this. The common law allows a Bishop to permit such celebration of mass *per modum actus.*[34]

THE FORCE OF "WORDS" IN GENERAL, AND CONSEQUENTLY, IN A PRIVILEGE.

Words are signs.[35] They give testimony of thought, and show the disposition of will. From their nature, words must serve the intention and *vice versa.* Barbosa compares words to the body and the mind to the soul. The former depends upon the latter for its activity.[36] Ordinarily words will show exactly what is present in the mind. This is the reason why words must be interpreted according to their proper meaning. In a privilege they have the same function.

---

32 Can. 68.

33 St. Alphonsus, *o.c.*, lib. I, app. II, c. I, n. 6; Suarez, *o.c.*, lib. 8, c. 28, n. 2; Vermeersch-Creusen, *o.c.*, v. I, n. 132; DeMeester, *o.c.*, n. 307.

34 Can. 822, § 4.

35 Grandclaude, *Breviarium Phil. Schol.*, (Parisiis, 1878), t. I, p. I, n. 27.

36 Barbosa, *Tractatus varii, Axiomata*, CCXXII, n. 3.

It happens at times that words are not precise and do not definitely convey the thought which they should express. Again, words which were once clear and unmistakable may lose these characteristics and take on an indefinite meaning. In order to assist in arriving at a practical conclusion in the interpretation of a given document the following rules are proposed. The general rules offered will govern all cases; the particular rules must be applied according to species of favor conceded.

General Rules. I. Briefly the first general principle of interpretation of a privilege may be expressed thus: *Privilegium tantum valet, quantum sonat.* The wording of a privilege is to be taken in its natural, or in its juridical sense.[37] This is the ordinary rule. However, if a word taken its proper meaning causes injustice to another, the legislator is not presumed to have used the word in that sense. Similarly, if the wording of a document shows clearly that a word was used improperly, this improper meaning evidently is not the idea which the legislator wishes to convey. Again, if the exact meaning of a word would render the privilege useless, manifestly the legislator does not intend it to have such a meaning.[38] The juridical meaning of a word is to be preferred to the natural meaning, if the two should not coincide.[39] The practice of the respective curia from which the document emanated is to be followed. Hence a Papal privilege is to be interpreted according to the use of the word in the Papal curia, and an Episcopal privilege according to the use of the word in the Episcopal curia.

II. If the rescript contains obscure or uncertain words, the doubt can be solved (a) by appealing to the

37 Suarez, *o.c.*, lib. 8, c. 28, n. 16; De Camillus, *Institutiones Iuris Canonici*, (Parisiis, 1868) lib. II, c. I, art. I, n. VI.

38 Schmalzgrueber, *o.c.*, lib. V, tit. XXXIII, n. 120; Fagnanus, *o.c.*, *de privilegiis et excessibus privilegiatorum, c. Quod nonnulla*, n. 28; Ballerini, *o.c.*, v. I, n. 391, I.

39 Schmalzgrueber, *o.c.*, lib. V, tit. XXXIII, n. 121.

petition, (b) by ascertaining how the privilege was interpreted in the beginning, (c) by considering the matter of the privilege, (d) by considering the quality of the privilege.[40]

(a) In granting his rescript, the legislator, or Superior is influenced by the petition offered. Hence ordinarily the Superior can reasonably be understood to grant the privilege in the same fashion in which it was requested.[41] Should a privilege be asked for to say mass on board ship, and the petition state that the request covers the period of two or three months necessary for an extended voyage, the legislator, if he accedes to the request, doubtless wishes to grant the privilege for so long a time. Similarly, if the request is made for a single trip to Europe, it would mean a round-trip.

In a *motu proprio* privilege, a petition is not the cause of the rescript altho it may be its occasion. Doubtful expressions occurring in such a rescript would have to be judged according to the following principles.

(b) In the course of time doubts may arise concerning words which at first seemed to be clear. In such a case it will be necessary to see how the privilege was interpreted in the beginning.[42] The immediate beneficiaries were in an excellent position to study the mind of the legislator and weigh all the circumstances incident to the issuance of the privilege. For example, if a privilege of having mass celebrated in a private oratory exists for some years, and now a doubt should arise about the admittance of certain people, sufficient security can be obtained by learning what the original grantee did.

(c) The substance of a privilege can very often dispel a doubt concerning the terms of a privilege.[43]

---

40 Grandclaude, *o.c.*, lib. V, sec. 3, n. 1.

41 Herincx, *o.c.*, disp. 4, q. 7, n. 88; Palao, *o.c.*, tr. 3, disp. 4, p. 9, n. 1; Suarez, *o.c.*, lib. 8, c. 28, n. 19.

42 Suarez, *o.c.*, *l.c.*

43 Suarez, *o.c.*, *l.c.*

Along some lines the legislator is accustomed to be generous, and along others not so favorable.

(d) The law to which a privilege might refer can also aid in interpreting a privilege. Privileges contrary to the law must be interpreted strictly:[44] privileges beyond the law can receive a broad interpretation.

Most of these suggestions are intrinsic to the rescript itself. Another, but an extrinsic guide might be added. Privileges granted to other persons than the immediate grantee can also serve as a source of interpretation.[45] In a given set of circumstances, the legislator is accustomed to grant privileges in the same way. Consequently, if one privilege seems obscure, it could be interpreted by reference to other privileges granting the same favor. Yet this means of interpretation may be precarious rule to follow at times since any warrantable circumstance may influence the legislator to concede his favors more or less generously. Prudence will demand a minute examination of both privileges in order to use similarity as a guide of interpretation.

Lastly, a privilege must not be interpreted in such a way that it becomes burdensome to the grantee. An interpretation of this kind would be more of an onus than a favor.[46] In regard to all the suggestions given above, the chief element of a privilege must be kept in mind. A privilege grants a concession. All interpretations must preserve this element.

Particular rules. Besides the general rules outlined above, a particular rule can be laid down for *favorable* privileges, and another rule for *odious* privileges.

I. *Favorable* or *gracious* privileges are privileges which cause no injury to common law, or prejudice to a third party. Numbered among such privileges would be

44 Cf. canons 19, 50, 85.

45 Suarez, *o.c.*, *l.c.*

46 Craisson, *o.c.*, v. I, n. 167.

indulgences, but not necessarily every kind of privilege beyond the law. The substance of a favorable privilege may be any kind of favor, material or spiritual. Since the favor alone is concerned, without reference to anything else, it receives a *broad* interpretation. One of the Rules of Boniface VIII[47] supplies the foundation for such broad interpretation: *favores convenit ampliari.* The word *convenit* is apt. A legislator should show himself beneficent whenever possible. Concessions that cannot do any harm go far toward conciliating minds which are not always tractable. Remunerative privileges, for instance, exhibit a sense of appreciation which may inspire further effort. Therefore, the widest possible interpretation is to be given to such favors, provided, of course, the interpretation remains within the proper meaning of the words.

*Motu proprio* privileges, even if they are against the common law, are to be interpreted widely. The reason is that the legislator, knowing the full content of common law, grants a concession which he could restrict if he desired. Since he does not restrict the terms of the privilege, he is presumed to incline toward a broad interpretation of the favor he has granted.[48]

II. *Odious* privileges regularly receive a *strict* interpretation.[49] A privilege can be odious in two ways. It may derogate from a law, or a custom; or, it may prejudice the rights of a third person.

Laws are for the common good. Hence any injury to a law, is an injury to the common law and therefore to be restricted as much as possible.[50] It will not avail to object that a privilege contrary to the law is a favor.

---

47 R. J. 15 in VI.

48 C. 23, *de praebendis et dignitatibus*, III, 4 in VI; Suarez, *o.c.*, lib. 8, c. 27, n. 8.

49 Grandclaude, *o.c.*, lib. V, sec. 3, n. 3; Makee, *o.c.*, v. I, n. 317.

50 Herincx, *o.c.*, disp. 4, q. 7, n. 89; Fagnanus, *o.c.*, *de privilegiis et excessibus privilegiatorum*, c. *Quod nonnulla*, n. 26.

While this is true in regard to the grantee, nevertheless such privileges are odious in respect of the law itself.[51] Since the law is to be favored more than any advantage accruing to a particular person as a result of an interpretation of his privilege, it follows that such an exception to the law must be interpreted in a way that the law can least suffer.[52] However, as Reiffenstuel[53] observes, and the Code itself demands, the essential note of a privilege must always be preserved.

Prejudice of rights can be considered in regard to the legislator himself whose rights are curtailed, or in regard to a third person who might suffer injury. Against the rights of the legislator a wide interpretation is allowed because he is believed to yield his rights according to the stipulations of the privilege. Besides, prejudice of this kind is almost intrinsic to every concession.[54] An exception requiring strict interpretation must be made in favor of privileges granted *ab Ecclesia Romana.*[55] Prejudice of the rights of the legislator is never presumed here.

Prejudice offered to the rights of a third person is always injurious, and therefore to be minimized as far as possible.[56] *Odia sunt restringenda.*[57] Thus Boniface VIII in restoring a benefice demanded that it be conferred without prejudice to the former incumbent.[58] The same Pontiff is explicit in dealing with the fruits of a benefice. The beneficiary does indeed enjoy the fruits of his benefice, but other possible beneficiaries, either by law, or by custom or privilege must be taken care of: *Intentionis nostrae nequaquam existit, si fructus huius-*

---

51 Suarez, *o.c.*, lib. 8, c. 27, n. 2.

52 C. 8, X, *de consuetudine,* I, 4; Suarez, *o.c.*, lib. 8, c. 27, n. 5.

53 Reiffenstuel, *o.c.*, lib. V, tit. XXXIII, n. 137.

54 Suarez, *o.c.*, lib. 8, c. 27, n. 4.

55 Fagnanus, *o.c.*, *de verborum significatione,* c. *olim,* n. 15-17.

56 Ferraris, *o.c.*, v. privilegium, art. 2, n. 28.

57 R. J. 15 in VI.

58 C. 8, *de rescriptis,* I, 3 in VI; cf. c. 15, X, *de officio et potestate iudicis delegati,* I, 29.

*modi, ecclesiae tuae fabricae vel alteri usui, seu cuicumque singulari personae de speciali consuetudine, privilegio vel statuto forsitan debeantur, quod eis per concessionem ipsam, nisi hoc expresse caveatur in ea, praeiudicium aliquod generetur.*[59]

The rule *minimum est sequendum* is true in most cases.[60] Fagnanus wisely says: *privilegium civiliter, et temperate est intelligendum, ita ut quanto minus fieri possit, iuri alieno praeiudicet.*[61]

### *Exceptions to the particular rule concerning odious privileges.*

An exception in regard to odious privileges can be made in favor of a community, or a pious cause, or even of a State. Because of the importance of the work which the beneficiaries perform, compensation for the injury offered the law will be had.[62]

While it is true that the rights in danger of being prejudiced by the use of odious privileges come from the legislator, and depend upon his will for their conservation, yet, ordinarily, these rights can hardly be considered subject to prejudice unless a specific mention to that effect is made. Such specific mention would be present in a privilege granted *ex certa scienta.* Undoubtedly this kind of a privilege would receive a wide interpretation even if the rights of a third party were prejudiced. The reason is evident. A privilege granted *ex certa scientia* is conceded with full knowledge of the circumstances, not only in connection with the grantee, but also in regard to possible restrictive consequences of inter-

59 C. 10, *de rescriptis,* I, 3 in VI; cf. c. 24, *de praebendis et dignitatibus,* III, 4, in VI.
60 R.J. 30 in VI.
61 Fagnanus, *o.c., de verborum significatione,* c. *olim,* n. 18.
62 St. Alphonsus, *o.c.,* lib. I, app. II, c. I, n. 8; Suarez, *o.c.,* lib. 8, c. 27, n. 7; Grandclaude, *o.c.,* lib. V, sec. 3, n. 1; D'annibale, *o.c.,* v I, n. 228; Ballerini, *o.c.,* v. I, n. 391, II.

ested persons. Similarly, a privilege, *motu proprio* provided it contain the proper clauses, receives a wide interpretation even if thru it a third person's rights are curtailed.[63]

*Perpetuity of a Privilege.*

Finally, a privilege is considered to be perpetual unless it is proven to be otherwise. Either the document itself will show the temporary force of the privilege, or the duration of the privilege will be determined at the time it is given *vivae vocis oraculo.* If in neither case a stipulation is made as to definite time of cessation, the privilege must be considered to be perpetual. Innocent III decided this in a response to the Archbishop of London. A predecessor of the incumbent Ordinary had granted a privilege to the monks of All Saints. No stipulation of time was made. The Archbishop entreated Rome to declare whether or not this privilege could continue. The Pope replied thus: *Si decimarum illarum remissio facta exstitit secundum canonicas sanctiones, praedecessor tuus indefinite decimas episcopales monasterio remittendo, quum nihil exceperit et poterit excepisse, ac in beneficiis plenissima sit interpretatio adhibenda, nec debeat una cademque substantia diverso iure censeri, intellexisse videtur non solum de decimis possessionum illius temporis, sed futuri.*[64]

Boniface VIII incorporated a similar declaration in his rules of law. Rule 16 reads: *Decet concessum a principe beneficium esse mansurum.* It is necessary, however, to note that the concession must have actually been made, else it would fail of realization if the grantor lost his power.[65]

The motive of a privilege will influence its stability.[66]

63 Herincx, *o.c.*, disp. 4, q. 7, n. 90.
64 C. 22, X, *de privilegiis et excessibus privilegiatorum*, V, 33.
65 C. 36, *de praebendis et dignitatibus*, III, 4 in VI.
66 DeMeester, *o.c.*, n. 305.

If a privilege were granted irrespective of its continued existence, the privilege would be in force even after the motive ceased. But if the continuance of the motive were taken into consideration, the privilege would be suspended when its motive ceased. This shows the similarity of certain privileges and certain dispensations in actual operation.[67]

Personal privileges even if they are relatively perpetual cease with the death of the grantee. Real privileges, however, pass to heirs and successors.[68]

---

[67] Grandclaude, *o.c.*, in regulas Sexti, n. 16.

[68] DeMeester, *o.c.*, l.c., *Cum rei inhaereat, transit hoc privilegium ad heredes et successores in eadem re.*

## CHAPTER VI

## USE OF A PRIVILEGE.

In discussing the use of a privilege a double aspect of the question must be considered. The use of a privilege can be viewed in relation to the privileged person himself, or in relation to all others who must respect the legitimate use of the privilege.[1] While this obligation is an effect of the concession, its prime force is rather to be sought in that principle of natural law whereby no one is allowed to interfere with the rights of another.

Consideration of the use of a privilege in respect of the grantee, easily resolves itself into a study of the time when a privilege may be used, and of the place where it may be enjoyed. Each division may be further subdivided. The element of time may be studied as perpetual or temporary, while the element of place may be considered in regard to the territory of the Holy Father, or of a Bishop.

Such favorable laws which are called privileges in a wide sense take effect at the time designated by the legislator. They need promulgation like any other law but they do not require acceptance. Hence the legitimate fruition of such a privilege begins when the law takes effect, continues as long as the law exists, and ceases when the law is revoked.

Strict privileges, on the other hand, are not of themselves laws. Consequently, they need no promulgation. Ordinarily the privilege does not take effect until the beneficiary accepts the grant. Formal acceptance is not essential. It suffices to have made a petition either in

1 Maroto, *o.c.*, v. I, n. 300.

person, or by proxy. As soon as the petition is granted, the privilege can be used. A priest who fears that total blindness is coming upon him can ask the Holy See for the privilege of celebrating the votive mass of the Blessed Virgin every day. Some time will be consumed in forwarding the petition to Rome. More time will be consumed there in investigation. Should the privilege be granted, it can be used validly at the moment of concession. It would not be necessary for the priest formally to accept the rescript when it is sent to him. Virtual acceptance is already had in the petition. Another case: a diocesan institute wishes to gain a plenary indulgence on certain specified days. The Bishop in his *ad limina* visit asks the Holy Father for the privilege. Immediately upon the concession of the Holy Father made thru the proper channels,[2] the institute receives its privilege.

The use of a privilege continues according to the stipulations of the grant. If the privilege is granted without reference to time, it can be used forever. But if a certain length of time is incorporated into the grant, the use of the privilege is valid until this time lapses. Besides the limitation of time, the specification of a certain number of cases can restrict the use of the privilege. Should the number be exceeded, the grantee would be acting invalidly.[3]

In regard to the place where a privilege may be used two general and self-evident principles can be proposed: (a) an absolute privilege can be used in every place in the territory of the grantor; (b) a privilege restricted to a certain place, or forbidden to be used in certain localities can only be enjoyed within the limits of the grant.

From the first principle it follows that a privilege granted by the Pope can be enjoyed everywhere. The

[2] Can. 258, § 2.

[3] In the internal forum, acts placed through inadvertence, *elapso tempore vel exhausto numero casuum*, are valid; can. 207, § 2.

Pope possesses jurisdiction everywhere and, consequently, he can concede a privilege which must be honored in all places. Bishops, however, do not enjoy universal jurisdiction. As a result in the matter of their own laws they can grant a privilege which will have force ordinarily only in the territory subject to them. The details of a privilege which follow the second principle named above must be learned from the grant itself. Thus if a Papal privilege allows a priest to celebrate mass on a portable altar, except where a church is within easy access, it would be unlawful to use this privilege in any other way. Or, if a Bishop should grant a privilege in a matter of his own law, but restrict the use to a certain city, it would be improper to extend the use of this privilege to another place. When the efficient cause of a privilege is well considered, the reason for these principles will be found readily. The efficient cause of a privilege is the legislator's will. This he can restrict or extend as he desires, and accordingly, the use of a privilege will be lawful or unlawful in so far as it agrees with the will of the legislator.

An interesting question arises at this point whether or not, under special circumstances, a privilege can be used beyond the territory of the grantor. It is hardly necessary to limit expressly this consideration to Episcopal privileges. From the very nature of the question Papal privileges are excluded since the Pope's jurisdiction exists everywhere, and knows no territorial limit. A Bishop's jurisdiction is limited by distinct territorial lines, and beyond these he has no jurisdiction. At first sight, then, it would seem that an Episcopal privilege could not be enjoyed outside of the grantor's diocese. However, if the idea of jurisdiction is further examined, it will be found that contentious jurisdiction[4] is limited

---

[4] *Contentiosa, iuxta omnes, iurisdictio dicitur quae controversias inter contendentes dirimit. Proinde necessario iudicialem processum requirit.* Solieri, *o.c.*, n. 47; cf. Can. 201, § 2.

to the confines of the diocese while voluntary jurisdiction[5] is not thus limited. For instance, a Bishop can grant faculties to priests in his diocese while he himself may be miles away from the diocese. So much is clear: a Bishop absent from his diocese can exercise voluntary jurisdiction in the diocese. But could Episcopal jurisdiction always be extended to validate the use of a privilege when the grantee himself were outside the diocese?

While the question presents some interesting features, it is not of much practical importance. If it be remembered that a Bishop has ordinary power to grant privileges only in respect of his own laws, the field is considerably narrowed. Excluding delegated power there can be no question of a privilege in the matter of a general law in so far as any Superior under the Pope is concerned. Then, if it be further remembered that most of the Episcopal laws are territorial and have no binding force beyond the diocese, the case becomes even more restricted. The question, then, resolves itself into a matter of a personal privilege. Maroto[6] says that such a privilege could be used outside of the diocese. Palao,[7] writing several centuries before, held the same view but hedged in his conclusion with so many restrictions that the privilege would seldom be enjoyed. Palao says that a privilege could be used outside the territory of the grantor provided it be not forbidden by common law, or by synodal law. Besides if the privilege were contrary to the existing law for contracts, or contrary to the common good, it could not be used. Modern ecclesiastical law dissolves one item of Palao's contention and confirms the rest. Canon 14, § 1, n. 2 says that travellers are not bound by the law of the place in which they are at pres-

[5] *Iurisdictio voluntaria dicitur qua Praelatus extraiudicialiter nemine contradicente, praebet officium, prouti si Ordines conferat, a censuris absolvat, indulgentias largiatur; vel etiam censuras per modum praecepti irrogat.* Solieri, *o.c.*, n. 47; cf. Can. 201, § 3.

[6] Maroto, *o.c.*, n. 300, v. I.

[7] Palao, *o.c.*, tr. 3, disp. 4, p. 6, n. 4-5.

ent unless these laws pertain to public order, or the solemnity of acts. Consequently, synodal laws do not bind travellers provided they do not govern matter allowed by the Code. Suarez's doctrine is much the same as that given by Palao. After pointing out that Papal privileges are of value everywhere, if they are conceded absolutely, Suarez applies the principle of territorial jurisdiction to prelates inferior to the Pope.[8] To use a privilege, says Suarez,[9] outside the territory where it was conceded, the matter of the privilege must not be forbidden by common law, or by particular law, and it must not depend on the consent of the Superior of the place where the grantee wishes to use his privilege. Suarez admits that a person can scarcely be enjoying a privilege when his activity is not forbidden. No privilege is needed where no law is infringed.

What conclusion can be drawn from these opinions? Maroto's brief statement that a personal privilege granted by a Bishop is valid everywhere, seems to be the only conclusion possible. The whole discussion is practically barren of examples because Episcopal laws are usually territorial laws, and have no force outside of the legislator's territory. But a Bishop can enact personal laws. These laws would bind even outside of the legislator's territory. An exemption from these laws would be valid everywhere. Canon 201, § 3 recognizes the power of jurisdiction to be exercised over an absentee subject: *Nisi aliud ex rerum natura aut ex iure constet, potestatem iurisdictionis voluntariam seu non-iudicialem quis exercere potest******* aut in subditum e territorio absentem.*

It is possible that a Bishop may enjoy delegated power to grant a privilege in respect of universal law. While this in effect might be considered a dispensation, its perpetuity would entitle it to be considered after the

---

8 Suarez, *o.c.*, lib. 8, cap. 26, n. 5.
9 Suarez, *o.c.*, lib. 8, cap. 26, n. 10.

manner of a privilege. For example, a Bishop using his delegated power grants one of his subjects a privilege not to fast.[10] Would this be of value outside the grantor's territory? Suarez[11] gives three reasons why such a privilege would be valid: (a) use considers the privilege to be valid; (b) the general law does not depend on one or the other place: a privilege simply removes the obligation without reference to territory; (c) congruity demands such interpretation, for the grantee has already been judged worthy of a privilege, and it would be difficult and arduous to go thru the same formalities whenever the grantee found himself in another diocese. Palao,[12] on the other hand, mentions an argument in opposition to such use of a privilege. The general law, he says, is physically one, but morally a distinct obligation in every place. This is shown from the fact that a custom may abrogate a law in one place while the obligation continues in another. Hence it cannot be inferred that a release from an obligation in one diocese, releases likewise from the obligations existing in other dioceses. Palao[13] himself answers this argument satisfactorily. Conceding the distinct obligation in every diocese, Palao maintains that the exemption, or privilege is really given by the supreme legislator himself, altho the concession is made by means of the grantee's Prelate. This seems to be the only proper response to the argument. The only way in which an inferior Prelate can grant a privilege in common law is by delegation. Delegation means that a person acts in the name of another. In this case it is the Superior who grants the power. According to the

---

10 Canon 1245 gives Ordinaries and pastors power to dispense in individual cases. The difference between this concession and the delegation considered in the text is obvious.

11 Suarez, *o.c.*, lib. 8, cap. 26, n. 15.

12 Palao, *o.c.*, tr. 3, disp. 4, p. 6, n. 7.

13 Palao, *o.c.*, tr. 3, disp. 4, p. 6, n. 8.

Rule of law,[14] it is the same to act thru another as to act oneself. Thus it may be said that the supreme legislator really grants the privilege, and consequently attributes validity wherever the law is in force. Two of Suarez's arguments are not conclusive. Use and congruity could scarcely of themselves solve the question at hand. However, Suarez's second argument is worthy of attention. It rests on legal principles and touches the point in discussion. Without needless repetition it can be seen that Suarez's reason is the same fundamentally as Palao's and receives similar confirmation from Rule 72 of Sexto.

The Code says a personal privilege follows the person.[15] This refers primarily to a personal privilege granted by the supreme legislator himself, but it also refers to personal privileges which are granted in his name. Therefore a personal privilege granted by a Bishop in virtue of his delegated power would be valid everywhere: *privilegium personale personam sequitur.*

There is scarcely any necessity to dilate on the territorial use of local privileges. Such privileges are attached to a determined place and cannot be used elsewhere. Thus a privilege of a votive mass at a shrine cannot be used except where the shrine exists.

There are several other points to be examined in the use of a privilege. It is possible that two privileges may exist in regard to a similar right. Again, one person may have the privilege to exact something, e. g., tithes, from everyone in his territory, and another person may enjoy the privilege of exemption from this tribute. In such circumstances which privilege is preferred? The first case is not difficult to solve. The concessions are parallel and should not conflict. Any opposition which may arise is entirely incidental and would not deprive one or the other of his rights. When communication of privi-

---

14 R.J. 72 in VI: *Qui facit per alium, est perinde, ac si faciat per se ipsum.*

15 Can. 74.

leges was in vogue, it was well within reason that apparent conflict might be had. Now, however, since this method of acquiring privileges is no longer in force,[16] less apparent opposition will be experienced.

But there is a case where a conflict of privileges really exists. This is what is formally known as *usus privilegii contra alium pariter privilegiatum.*[17] In this case a conflict exists in regard to the use of the same privilege. The example of tithes will help to bring the details of this conflict of rights. A Bishop obtains the privileges of exacting tithes from everyone in his territory. At the same time there exists a privilege that a certain religious institute is exempt from tithes. Obviously, one right cannot be secured without the sacrifice of the other.

The rule which might be advanced, *privilegiatus non potest uti privilegio suo contra alium privilegiatum,* is unsatisfactory, as Schmalzgrueber himself admits.[18] The reason is that no matter what the rule may say in a general way, one of the privileged parties ordinarily preserves his privilege intact. While a rule cannot be expected to hold for every individual case, yet it should cover the majority of cases, and certainly be a general standard which can be invoked to settle disputes. Hence more detailed principles are necessary in order to arrive at a suitable conclusion for all questions concerning a conflict in the use of privileges.

(a) In the first place, after noting possible irritating clauses, it is necessary to examine the scope of the conflicting privileges. If one privilege is general, and the other particular, the latter is to be preferred to the former because it is a derogation of it.[19] Therefore,

---

16 Inability to acquire privileges by communication is restricted to religious. Cf. can. 613, § 1.

17 Schmalzgrueber, *o.c.*, lib. V, tit. XXXIII, n. 100-105.

18 Schmalzgrueber, *o.c.*, lib. V, tit. XXXIII, n. 105.

19 R.J. 34 in VI; Suarez, *o.c.*, lib. 8, cap. 23, n. 6; Palao, *o.c.*, tr. 3, disp. 4, p. 8, n. 2; Tuschus, *o.c.*, v. VI, concl. 760, n. 13.

using the example above, if the Bishop's privilege was so general as to cover every person and institute in his diocese, while the institute's privilege merely regarded exemption from Episcopal tithes, then the institute can enjoy its privilege to the loss of the Bishop's rights.

(b) Secondly, if both privileges are particular, or both general, the privilege ought to be inspected to see if there is some way to conciliate both.[20] Verbal conflict may be had without real opposition. Some condition may not be apparent at first sight, but would be revealed upon closer examination.

(c) Thirdly, if the privileges really conflict, the privilege to be enjoyed will be the one which is stronger in law. Thus priority of concession will determine which one is to be used:[21] or, the position held by the grantor will solve the difficulty. A Papal privilege will take preference over an Episcopal privilege.[22]

The rule, then, that a privileged person cannot use his privilege against another privileged person must be correctly understood to mean that the former cannot prosecute his rights against a stronger right. It matters little how this prevalence is shown.[23] Should it be impossible to detect any prevalence, both privileges must be referred to their grantor for further consideration. The Code says, in the case of rescripts, both are invalid if priority cannot be established.[24]

Passing from the consideration of the positive use of a privilege it remains to be seen whether a privilege must be used. If it be remembered that a privilege consists in the concession of a favor and the right to use this favor, hardly any obligation can be urged to force the use of a privilege. But it must be further borne

20 Schmalzgrueber, *o.c.*, lib. V, tit. XXXIII, n. 102.
21 Can. 48, § 2.
22 Schmalzgrueber, *o.c.*, lib. V, tit. XXXIII, n. 103.
23 Schmalzgrueber, *o.c.*, lib. V, tit. XXXIII, n. 105.
24 Can. 48, § 3.

in mind that only the gratuitous nature of a favor is now considered, apart from any necessity arising from duty, or precept. Hence with one stroke many privileges widely so-called, or real laws, are eliminated from this discussion as common law demands their use.[25] Thus, for instance a priest cannot forego the use of his *privilegium canonis*, or *fori*. Similarly an exempt religious could not neglect to use his privilege of exemption from Episcopal jurisdiction. Canon 69 defines the issue very well:

**Canon 69. Nemo cogitur uti privilegio in sui dumtaxat favorem concesso, nisi alio ex capite exsurgat obligatio.**

The first part of this canon is explicit. Alexander III in his answer to the monks of Saint Andrew's monastery says any one is free to yield his rights.[26] The Rules of Law contain an axiom which is applicable here. Rule 61 says *Quod ob gratiam alicuius conceditur, non est in eius dispendium retorquendum.* A favor should not turn out to be harmful; and, therefore, if this development is feared, the favor need not be used.

An obligation to use a privilege may arise from a cause extraneous to the privilege. For example, a privilege may be enjoyed in regard to attending mass during an interdict. Should the grantee of such a privilege reside in a locality where an interdict is in force, he would be obliged to fulfill the precept of the Church. The reason for this obligation is that a precept exists *de facto* since the effect of the censure is removed by means of a privilege. Thus observance of the precept is licit for the privileged person while it would be illicit for the community under the interdict. Hence the privileged person would be obliged to use his privilege in order

---

25 Zoesius, *o.c.*, lib. V, tit. XXXIII, n. 28.

26 C. 6, X, *de privilegiis et excessibus privilegiatorum*, V, 33.

that he could fulfill the law of the Church.[27] Generally speaking, the same obligation arises to use a privilege whenever by means of a privilege an obstacle is removed permitting the fulfillment of law or precept.[28]

Palao[29] and Suarez[30] question the statement that, strictly speaking, a privileged person can be obliged to use his privilege if it be conceded merely in his own favor. For instance, from a consideration of the favor granted in the privilege discussed in the preceding paragraph, it is clear that the privilege removes the effect of the censure, but does not touch any duties that the grantee may have. The wording of Canon 69 does not directly reprehend this opinion, altho it places the obligation more on the use of the privilege rather than on a possible effect the use might have. The principal objection to Palao's and Suarez's opinion is that it does not allow for those privileges the purpose of which is not to exempt the grantee from the effect of penalties. Any number of privileges exist in which the actual positive use of a privilege is necessary. Many privileges beyond the law are of this kind: such as the faculty of absolving from reserved sins, etc. It cannot be said that the privi-

27 Suarez, *o.c.*, lib. 8, cap. 23, n. 8.

28 Schmalzgrueber, *o.c.*, lib. V, tit. XXXIII, n. 99. Bucceroni, (*Casus Conscientiae*, 21, 1) admits that a privilege which exempts from a censure must be used because the common law enjoins a precept, but he denies that a privilege must be used in other instances. Thus a privilege to hear mass in a private oratory would not have to be used by a person who could not leave the house. One of Bucceroni's reasons is that celebration of mass in a private oratory is "*quid odiosum.*" While this may be true in respect of the place where mass is to be celebrated, it hardly touches the obligation arising from precept. Bucceroni's second reason is of more value. A privilege to hear mass in a private oratory does not immediately affect the impediment, *e.g.*, infirmity, and hence does not call for active use of the privilege. Yet the obligation of the precept seems to cancel the freedom which would attend the use of the privilege, assuming that no great inconvenience arises. Therefore, if mass could be had without great inconvenience, the precept would have to be fulfilled. Cf. Noldin, *o.c.*, n. 195.

29 Palao, *o.c.*, tr. 3, disp. 4, p. 7, n. 2-3.

30 Suarez, *o.c.*, lib. 8, cap. 23, n. 9.

lege exempts from these reservations, and thus common law would apply. On the contrary a formal use of the privilege would be necessary in order that it may have effect.

Can this formal use of a privilege be of obligation? Canon 69 expressly states that such an obligation can arise. The common good, as Maroto[31] observes, together with possible private injury might make the use of a privilege obligatory. A penitent may confess reserved sins to a confessor who enjoys the faculty of absolving from such sins. Injury to the penitent would result if the confessor refused to use his privilege. Hence he would be obliged to absolve the reserved sins.[32]

Aside from any extrinsic obligation which may arise restricting the freedom conceded in the use of a privilege, canon 69 limits the liberty of using or not using a privilege to those privileges which are granted solely in favor of the grantee. A person may enjoy a privilege without its concession having been made directly to himself. Such a privilege must be used whenever a legitimate occasion presents itself. For purposes of clarity, it will be well to distinguish between the privileges resulting from common law, and the privileges accruing from particular law.

(a) Common law contains among others[33] two important classes of privileges: clerical privileges and exemption. The latter is less extensive than the former, for according to canon 615 it affects only those religious who are regulars. Their novices are included. Any other religious society must receive special concession

---

31 Maroto, *o.c.*, n. 300; cf. Smith, *o.c.*, n. 127.

32 Vermeersch-Creusen, *o.c.*, v. I, n. 134; Genicot, *o.c.*, v. I, n. 109; St. Alphonsus, *o.c.*, lib. I, app. II, c. I, n. 3.

33 E.g., Cardinals, can. 239; Bishops, can. 349; Administrators, can. 315; Vicars and Prefects Apostolic, can. 308. The use of all of the privileges granted to Prelates cannot be urged with any obligation unless their rank would suffer from non-use of the privileges.

of the privilege of exemption.[34] Clerical privileges, however, include all who have at least received tonsure, and besides these, extends to all religious whether regular or not.[35] In considering these privileges, it must always be remembered that they are conceded to individual persons in view of their state in life. Of course, one of the practical effects of these privileges is to make the individual person privileged so that he may have protection and rights which he would not otherwise enjoy. With this in mind, it is easy to understand why a cleric, or a regular must always use his privilege. To fail to do so would work an injury to his respective state even tho in some particular interest he might fare better by a non-use of his privilege. For instance, a regular may be dissatisfied with the attitudes of his Superior. The Ordinary of the diocese, however, is more favorable. Revolving this in his mind, the regular considers it to be more advantageous should he not use his privilege of exemption, and thus place himself under the jurisdiction of the Ordinary of the diocese. This, however, he cannot do as his privilege is bound up with the rights of his Order. Any personal discomfort will not justify the sacrifice of the community's rights.[36]

(b) Privileges resulting from particular law must likewise be used. While the reason is not the same as obtains in privileges granted to a state in life, yet the privilege does pertain to the community as such, and not to the individuals who comprise the community. Thus, for instance, a congregation obtains the privilege of reciting a proper office in honor of a saint. All the members of the congregation are obliged to recite this office and not the common one. Non-use of such a privilege would infringe on the rights obtained by the entire

---

34 Can. 618, § 1.
35 Can. 614.
36 Tuschus, *o.c.*, v. VI, concl. 759, n. 3.

community.[37] Similarly, a different form of election than that described in the Code must be used by all the members of the community to which it is conceded.

---

37 Vermeersch-Creusen, *o.c.*, v. I, n. 134.

## CHAPTER VII

## CESSATION OF PRIVILEGES.

In an earlier chapter it was admitted that the note of stability could be numbered among the few characteristics which a law and a privilege have in common.[1] Absolute stability will not be found in human legislation, whether ecclesiastical or civil, for such a degree of permanence postulates an immutable will of a legislator. Relative stability, however, is attainable. A greater relative stability will be found in a law than in a privilege for the reason that the common good counsels that a settled condition be not disturbed. But, as is evident, this settled condition can give place to a change in legislation whenever necessity demands such alteration of law. Thus abrogation, and derogation destroy the note of stability found in a law.[2]

In a privilege stability is also necessary because the particular good precludes indiscriminate and unreasonable destruction and alteration of rights.[3] Yet the stability of a privilege is subject to more changing circumstances than can effect a change in a law. Thus renunciation can cause the loss of a privilege as well as revocation. Other methods of losing a privilege, such as lapse of time, loss of power, etc., show that the stability of a privilege is not the same as the stability of a law.

A privilege can be lost either by the defect of some intrinsic condition or quality, or by the extrinsic action of a Superior.[4] In the former case, the privilege would cease of itself without any procedure on the part of the

---

1 Cf. p. 6.
2 Verméersch-Creusen, *o.c.*, v. I, n. 77.
3 R.J. 16 in VI.
4 Suarez, *o.c.*, lib. VIII, c. 29, n. 2.

competent authority. Thus, for instance, faculties for a limited number of cases cease when this number has been completed.[5] On the other hand, extrinsic action can terminate a privilege at any time even if the fruition of the privilege would still be beneficial.

The ways in which a privilege can be lost are many. The Code thru seven canons furnishes the underlying principles according to which the loss of a privilege must be judged. A more detailed exposition will be found in the following numbers.

### 1. *Revocation of Privileges.*

**Can. 71. Per legem generalem revocantur privilegia in hoc Codice contenta; ad cetera quod attinet, servetur praescriptum can. 60.**

Before entering upon an exposition of this canon, it may be well to enumerate the possible methods of revocation, adding a word of explanation. *Express revocation* is so evident that it needs no further elucidation. *Tacit revocation*, on the other hand, requires a little consideration. Perhaps the best way to explain tacit revocation would be to show how it may occur.

There are three ways in which *tacit revocation* may be had. First, by universal law. Following the reason laid down by Boniface VIII, individual grants are not included in the revocation made by universal law.[6] The legislator is presumed not to be acquainted with these individual grants, or privileges. Often enough they will be the result of custom concerning which the legislator would have, perhaps, only the imperfect knowledge which results from the legal assent accorded customs.[7] Secondly, by judicial sentence. A person may enjoy immunity by reason of a privilege, but if nevertheless he is

---

[5] Can. 207, § 2 is an exception to this principle.

[6] C. 1 *de constitutionibus*, I, 2 in VI.

[7] Can. 25, 63, § 1.

legitimately condemned, his privilege is considered revoked. Thirdly, by the concession of another, and possibly parallel privilege. But this would at most be a diminution of the former privilege rather than an absolute and general revocation.[8] These three items of tacit revocation are admittedly elastic and can scarcely give a certain indication of the altered mind of the legislator. But tacit revocation is a difficult subject to surround with definite rules. A negative rule would be almost as unsatisfactory. Yet this principle may be helpful in deciding cases: tacit revocation is not present in particular rescripts. Recognizing the difficulty of the question at hand, the legislator will generally make proper provision for the revocation of privileges, if he intends to revoke them. But this would already become express revocation.

It is fitting here to mention the rule which the Code proposes in order to judge the existence or non-existence of privileges in relation to the canons of the Code. Canon 4[9] gives this rule: in order that privileges may exist after the Code was published, it is necessary that the grant be conceded by the Holy See, that the beneficiary be a physical or moral person; that the privilege be still in use, and not revoked at some time in the past; and finally that the privilege be not expressly revoked by the Code itself.

Episcopal privileges are not affected by canon 4. These privileges will remain in force, or be revoked according to the prescription of canons 71 and 60, § 2.

In order that Papal privileges may enjoy the suffrage of canon 4, the privileges must actually be in use, that is, in legitimate use and not lost thru renunciation, or liberative prescription. The privileges must not have

---

8 Suarez, *o.c.*, lib. VIII, c. 39, n. 1, 2, 4, 5.

9 Can. 4. *Iura aliis quaesita, itemque privilegia atque indulta quae, ab Apostolica Sede ad haec usque tempora personis sive physicis sive moralibus concessa, in usu adhuc sunt nec revocata, integra manent, nisi huius Codicis canonibus expresse revocentur.*

been revoked before the Code. It does not follow, however, that such privileges may not be revoked after the Code. This, in fact, took place in a decree of the Congregation for the Propagation of the Faith, January 16, 1924.[10] The privilege of precedence was thus lost to missionaries who enjoyed the title "Apostolic Missionary." Finally, the privileges must not have revoked by the Code itself.[11] Examples of such revocation can be found in canons 343, § 2; 403; 460, § 2; 519; 522; 544, § 2; 654; 774, § 1; 876, § 1; 964, n. 1; 1157; 1356; 1576, § 1.

A decision of the Holy Office will give a practical illustration of canon 4. A question was thus proposed to the Holy Office: *Utrum post can.* 930[12] *novi Codicis adhuc perseveret existentia altaris privilegiati pro agonizantibus?* The Holy Office answered: *Affirmative.*

Similarly the Congregation for Religious decided that the privilege conceded to novices by the decree *Spirituali consolationi* still held its force. This privilege consisted in allowing novices who were in danger of death to make their religious profession, altho the requisite term for the novitiate had not been completed.[13]

With these introductory notions explained, canon 71 can be examined. The first part of this canon refers to privileges which are found in common law. While such privileges confer favors they do so by means of a law. Most of these favors are obtained only when all the elements of a law are present.[14] The beneficiary is not free to reject his privileges. In some cases, however, the grantee will not be obliged to use his privilege.

In order that these privileges may cease, the Code

10 AAS. v. XVI, p. 243.

11 Cicognani, *o.c.*, p. 27.

12 Can. 930. *Nemo indulgentias acquirens potest eas aliis in vita degentibus applicare; animabus autem in purgatorio detentis indulgentiae omnes a Romano Pontifice concessae, nisi aliud constet, applicabiles sunt.*

13 Both decisions in Cicognani, *o.c.*, p. 31.

14 ASS. v. III, p. 433.

postulates a general law. Of course, a single religion now enjoying the privilege of exemption may lose this favor by a disposition of the Holy See. But the effect would be merely to deprive this individual religion of its privilege without touching the privilege itself as it is contained in the Code.[15]

That a new general law revokes a former general law was already recognized by Boniface VIII.[16] He writes that a later constitution revokes the former. But he adds: *quamvis de ipsa mentionem non faciat.* Thus the mere incompatibility of the two general laws, covering the same matter argues the revocation of the former law.[17] Therefore, should a future law be enacted which, without reference to the privilege of exemption, state that henceforth all religious are to be subject to the Ordinary of the diocese, the privilege of exemption would cease by virtue of canon 71. This principle is applicable to all the favorable laws existing in the Code.

The second part of canon 71 is concerned with privileges in the strict sense of the word. While reference is made in the canon merely to rescripts, the same underlying juridical principles likewise have their application in verbal privileges. As it was observed above,[18] verbal privileges embody all the requisites of a privilege. In fact, favors granted by rescript, and concessions awarded verbally differ only in the non-essential element of writing. To revoke a verbal privilege a document is not necessary. The mere notification of the change in the legislator's will is sufficient to cause the loss of the privilege.[19]

---

15 Can. 615. *Regulares, novitiis non exclusis, sive viri sive mulieres, cum eorum domibus et ecclesiis, exceptis iis monialibus quae Superioribus regularibus non subsunt, ab Ordinarii loci iurisdictione exempti sunt, praeterquam in casibus a iure expressis.*

16 C. 1 *de constitutionibus,* I, 2 in VI.

17 DeCamillis, *o.c.,* lib. II, C. 1, art. I, n. XII.

18 Cf. p. 18.

19 Palao, *o.c.,* tr. 3 disp. 4, p. 21, § 5, n. 4.

The first principle of revocation laid down in the Code[20] says that a rescript that has been revoked by a special act of a Superior continues in force until the revocation has been intimated to the one who obtained the rescript. While this principle applies to all rescripts, its express application is made in canon 71 to the matter of privileges. Now if this principle be examined closely it will be found that the legislator extends the actual duration of a rescript from the time that he expresses his intention to revoke until the time that this intention is made known to the grantee.[21] In ecclesiastical law, the will of the legislator, requiring no consent of the governed, is powerful enough to bring a privilege into existence without waiting for acceptance of the favor. Thus a rescript can be granted, and is valid without the consent of the grantee.[22] A privilege enjoys the same priority because its entire efficient cause is the benign disposition of the legislator. Such is the principle which governs the issuance of a rescript, or privilege.

Revocation similarly lodges in the legislator's will.[23] What is conceded without consent can be revoked without consent. Therefore, if this element be stressed, it will be seen that, strictly speaking, a rescript can be revoked as soon as the legislator signifies his intention to do so. What is found, then, in canon 60, § 1, is nothing else than a suspension of the effect of the legislator's will until it be made known to the grantee. However, should the document of revocation read expressly that at the moment of intimation, the legislator chooses to revoke, then his intention would not be complete until the grantee is notified.

If the proper position of the legislator be further

---

20 Can. 60, § 1. *Rescriptum, per peculiarem Superioris actum revocatum, perdurat usque dum revocatio ei, qui illud obtinuit, significetur.*

21 Palao, *o.c.*, *l.c.*, n. 2 says this was the teaching in his day.

22 Can. 37.

23 Palao, *o.c.*, *l.c.*, n. 4.

kept in mind, no difficulty will arise concerning the necessity of a cause in order that a revocation of a privilege be valid. A just cause is not essential to the validity of a privilege. Neither, at least in a general way, is a just cause essential for the revocation of a privilege. The reason is that a privilege depends for its conservation as well as for its beginning on the benign will of the legislator. True enough, revocation without cause would be capricious and scarcely befitting a Superior. Nevertheless, should such revocation occur, it would be valid. The privilege would cease.

All this is true in its fullest sense in regard to privileges which refer to delegation; it is likewise true of revocation of all gracious privileges. But onerous and conventional privileges may not be so summarily revoked. A question of justice and mutual obligation arises in these privileges. Often these two classes of privileges will converge into one as happens in concordats.

It must be remembered that the question is not whether the Pope can revoke these privileges, but whether without cause he can revoke them. It seems that justice would be violated if the Pope did not have a sufficient cause for his revocation. The beneficiary assumed a burden which he would not have assumed if the privileges had not been granted to him. Therefore, since a reciprocal obligation exists, the privilege cannot be revoked without a just cause[24] unless the object of the privilege conceded should be a right which the Pope could not alienate. What would be such a cause for revocation? The public good will furnish such a cause.[25] The Pope is the judge of the necessity of the revocation and of the sufficiency of the cause. His decision would have to be followed. Compensation would have to be

24 Smith, *o.c.*, n. 129; Cf. Solieri, *o.c.*, n. 339.

25 Besides the common good, Calvinus suggests *delictum, abusus, iniquitas, cessatio causae finalis, necessitas, utilitas, o.c.*, ver. privilegium.

made to the former beneficiary but this could take many forms, such as, surrender of a corresponding benefit, or, substitution of another privilege less injurious to the common good.[26]

In revoking a privilege, liceity always demands a just cause. A Superior is presumed to act with prudence and thoughtfulness. He is always expected to propose to himself sufficient reasons for his actions. Hence to revoke a privilege licitly, a Superior must have a just cause, and one proportionate to the privilege he revokes. Maroto [27] observes the nice gradation of causes required for the revocation of a gracious, and a remunerative privilege. The latter is awarded in recognition of merit and postulates a weightier cause than expected for the revocation of a gracious privilege.

It may be recalled here that the first part of canon 71 deals with privileges which are contained in the Code. These were seen to be lost by the enactment of a contrary general law. The case is entirely different when a general law contrary to a strict privilege outside the Code is promulgated. The Code expressly states[28] that such a law does not revoke rescripts (privileges) unless the law itself declare that it does, or the law be given by one higher in authority than the Superior who issued the rescript.

Assuming a legitimate cause for liceity, it is evident that the legislator can revoke all individual grants opposed to his law.[29] But is he presumed to do so? Boniface VIII decided that a constitution did not abolish customs and statutes unless express mention were made.[30] Boniface VIII himself supplies an illustration of such express revocation. Abuses had arisen from

26 Palao, *o.c.*, *l.c.*, n. 1; Maroto, *o.c.*, v. I, n. 301.
27 Maroto, *o.c.*, *l.c.*
28 Can. 60, § 2.
29 Palao, *o.c.*, tr. 3, disp. 4, p. 21, § 3, n. 1.
30 C. 1, *de constitutionibus*, I, 2 in VI.

concessions granted to absentee beneficiaries. Divine worship was neglected and the clerics had at times even omitted the recitation of the Breviary which gave the title to their benefice. The Pope in one stroke revoked all these concessions. *Nos volentes emendare praeterita, et quantum possumus adversus futura cavere, omnes huiusmodi et similes indulgentias, personis, non ecclesiis vel dignitatibus datas, penitus revocamus, et earum concessionem nostris volumus exsulare temporibus.*[31]

The Code adopts this principle of Boniface VIII and applies it to rescripts. At first sight the full application of this principle does not seem to be in force at present for canon 60, § 2 does not demand express revocation. The canon reads: *nisi aliud in ipsa lege caveatur.* Thus tacit revocation seems to be admitted. This tacit revocation would happen if the wording of the law were contrary to the continued use of the privilege. However, if the first part of canon 71 be studied closely, it will be seen that only privileges existing universally come under the revocation of a general law. Individual rescripts and privileges are thereby unaffected. Therefore the clause *nisi aliud in ipsa lege caveatur* must be taken to mean express revocation. This could be obtained by the use of formulas such as *non obstantibus privilegiis; non obstantibus quibuscumque privilegiis etiam speciali mentione vel specialissima mentione dignis.*[32]

The norms treated here are likewise applicable to the revocation of Episcopal privileges, and rescripts. A Bishop can grant a privilege in regard to his own law, and can grant it in the form of a rescript. Now if he should found another law which would be contrary to the use of the rescript obtained under the former law, the Bishop would have to make special mention concerning revocation of rescripts and privileges in order that

31 C. 15, *de rescriptis*, I, 3 in VI.

32 Suarez, *o.c.*, lib. VIII, c. 38, n. 1-3; Maroto, *o.c.*, v. I, 301.

they might cease. If this special mention were omitted, the use of the rescript would be valid and lawful.

The last item to be considered under revocation of privileges illustrates the hierarchical jurisdiction of the Church. Canon 60, § 2 reads: *Per legem contrariam nulla rescripta revocantur, nisi****** aut lex lata sit a Superiore ipsius rescribentis.* Obviously, the application of this part of the canon is possible only in regard to Episcopal privileges or their equivalent in the face of a Pontifical law. The Pope has no superior on earth, and consequently there is no question of Papal privileges being revoked by a higher power. But the revocation of Episcopal privileges must come from a law made by a Superior, considered in the complete jurisdictional sense. Hence an Archbishop cannot revoke the privileges, or rescripts conceded by one of his Suffragan Bishops: nor can an Abbot Primate revoke the rescripts of one of the Abbots under his vigilance. Express revocation is not demanded. It suffices for revocation that the Papal law be so worded that an Episcopal privilege becomes contrary to this law.

### 2. *Renunciation of Privileges.*

**Can. 72. 1. Privilegia cessant per renunciationem a competente Superiore acceptam.**

**2. Privilegio in sui tantum favorem constituto quaevis persona privata renuntiare potest.**

**3. Concesso alicui communitati, dignitati, locove renuntiare privatis personis non licet.**

**4. Nec ipsi communitati seu coetui integrum est renuntiare privilegio sibi dato per modum legis, vel si renuntiatio cedat in Ecclesiae aliorumve praeiudicium.**

*Renunciation* is twofold: *proper* and *improper.* The latter consists in mere non-use. It is not a surrender of the power to act such as a privilege allows. For instance, a privilege to eat meat on days of abstinence is granted by the Holy Father. The beneficiary, knowing that he is now exempted from the law, nevertheless decides to abstain. This non-use of a privilege is called an improper renunciation of the privilege because it is concerned merely with the effect of the privilege without touching the power, or faculty conceded.[33] Proper renunciation, on the other hand, is the free surrender of the faculty conceded by the privilege.[34] In the example just given, should the beneficiary yield his right not to abstain from meat on forbidden days, there would be had proper renunciation. This assumes that the other condition, namely, acceptance on the part of the legitimate Superior, were fulfilled.

Besides this active surrender on the part of the beneficiary the renunciation of the privilege must be accepted by the competent Superior. The reason for this is that the concession, use, fruition, and loss of a privilege all depend upon the will of the Superior, or legislator. He it is who grants the privilege, and his will must undergo a change before the privilege can cease. The same principle holds, in general, in the renunciation of benefices.[35]

The competent Superior to accept renunciation will be the one who granted the privilege, or his delegate. Thus the Pope can accept the renunciation of a Papal privilege; the Bishop the renunciation of an Episcopal privilege. The Superior of a Bishop can likewise accept the renunciation of an Episcopal privilege. Yet it must be remembered here as well as in the revocation of privileges, that an Archbishop is not competent in regard to the privileges of his Suffragans, nor any other Superior

---

33 Suarez, *o.c.*, lib. VIII, c. 33, n. 3.

34 Schmalzgrueber, *o.c.*, lib. V, tit. XXXIII, n. 180; Palao, *o.c.*, tr. 3, disp. 4, p. 17, n. 5.

35 E.g., can. 157; 184; 191.

whose power is not in the direct and complete line of jurisdiction.

An objection answered by Palao, might be raised here.[36] In granting a privilege, the Superior usually does so with the tacit condition that the grantee accept the privilege, or concession. But by renunciation the grantee no longer accepts the privilege. Therefore, renunciation does not require acceptance on the part of the Superior. This objection would be valid if the condition implied at the time of the concession of the privilege could be understood to continue forever. If a privilege were granted in this way, no acceptance would be necessary. However, privileges are usually granted absolutely in this respect at least. Freedom is allowed for the initial acceptance of the grantee, and then the condition ceases. The will of the legislator is fulfilled as soon as the privilege is accepted. After that the Rule of Sexto Bonifacii VIII is in force: *Decet beneficium concessum a principe esse mansurum.*[37]

With the principle proposed in canon 72, § 1 understood, the following paragraphs of the canon can be considered.

At the risk of repetition, it must be stated again that a privilege can be considered personal in two ways: first, in so far as a privilege has its effect in an individual person, and second, in so far as a privilege has its entire being in the individual person. The second paragraph of canon 72 considers only the latter division. Therefore, only *privilegium singulariter personale,* or individually personal, is meant here. Innocent III in his letter to the Archbishop of Pisa implies the capacity of an individual person to renounce his personal privileges by condemning the custom of clerics in surrendering

---

36 Palao, *o.c., l.c.*, n. 7.
37 R.J. 16 in VI.

their *privilegium fori.*[38] Clement III expounded the law similarly in the case of a violation of *privilegium canonis.*[39] A cleric who had suffered at the hands of an aggressor received compensation for his injuries. Thus he intended to circumvent the provisions of law entailing excommunication. The Pope refused this renunciation of the privilege accorded the clerical state, and maintained that private compensation in no way superseded the law. Another case of the violation of *privilegium canonis* took place under the reign of Innocent III. In the diocese of Braga, a custom existed that clerics voluntarily subjected themselves to corporal punishment in satisfaction for injuries. Upon request of the Bishop whether this custom could continue, the Pope responded that even tho this were not a violent assault, yet it was injurious to the clerical state and hence forbidden.[40]

Gregory IX explicitly allowed the renunciation of personal privileges, altho this statement was only a secondary item connected with a natural right. In discussing the freedom of novices to return to the world, the Pope writes: *Statuimus, novitios in probatione positos ante susceptum religionis habitum, qui dari profitentibus consuevit, vel ante professionem emissam, ad priorem statum redire posse libere infra annum, nisi evidenter appareat, quod tales absolute voluerint vitam mutare et in religione perpetuo Domino deservire,* QUUM QUILIBET RENUNCIARE VALEAT EI, QUOD PRO SE NOSCITUR INTRODUCTUM.[41]

This principle of private renunciation of privileges is taken up in the Code, as well as the prohibition of private renunciation in connection with privileges accorded a state in life.[42]

38 C. 12, X, *de foro competenti,* II, 2.
39 C. 15, X, *de sententia excommunicationis,* V, 39.
40 C. 36, X, *de sententia excommunicationis,* V, 39.
41 C. 23, X, *de regularibus et transeuntibus ad religionem,* III, 31.
42 Can. 123.

A comparison of the first two paragraphs of canon 72 implies that a beneficiary can still enjoy his privilege even after he has made the formal act of renunciation.[43] Unless the renunciation were made personally to the competent Superior, and immediately accepted, some time would elapse between the renunciation of the privilege and its acceptance. During this time, the privilege is still in force and can be used validly. The reason for this is that the will of the legislator, or Superior is unaltered until he accepts the renunciation. This is clear enough from the nature of the case, but there is not wanting a Papal decision which supposes this principle. Boniface VIII thus determines the efficacy of delegation in regard to a procurator: *Licet is, qui procurator constituitur ab absente, dixerit, praesentatum sibi suscipere nolle mandatum: hoc tamen nequaquam obstante, quamdiu constituens in eadem persistiterit voluntate, ipsum acceptare poterit, quandocumque placebit.*[44]

In order to avoid needless repetition, this principle gathered from a comparison of the first and second paragraphs of canon 72 equally applies to the renunciation treated in paragraph 4 of this same canon.

A privilege which is held jointly by two or more grantees cannot be renounced by one of the beneficiaries, provided that the matter of the privilege is indivisible. One of the grantees is not allowed to prejudice the rights of his companions. However, if the privilege were really divisible so that the association of the beneficiaries were but nominal, and the grantees not at all considered as participants of the same numerical privilege, then each one individually could renounce his own rights.[45]

---

43 Reiffenstuel drew the same conclusion according to the law of his day, *o.c.*, lib. V, tit. XXXIII, n. 189.
44 C. 7, *de procuratoribus,* I, 19 in VI.
45 Palao, *o.c.,* tr. 3, disp. 4, p. 17, n. 1.

The third paragraph of canon 72 imposes a further restriction on private renunciation of privileges. From the texts of law cited, it is evident that private persons are not permitted to renounce the privileges accruing to them by reason of their state. But neither are they competent to renounce the privileges which do not result from a state in life, but are the rights of some community, dignity, or place. The Code enumerates these subjects of privilege. A few words concerning each one will help to understand the prohibition enjoined on private persons.

A community, such as a religious Order, or a Congregation may enjoy privileges. A number do enjoy faculties to give special blessings. Such privileges are granted to the community as a whole. All the members of the Order, or Congregation, provided they are priests, are usually empowered to use the privileges, but in doing so they are not exercising a right which pertains to them primarily. Now since the privilege is not individually personal, it cannot be renounced by the action of a private person.[46] True the privilege may not always be used, if the religious Superior allows this freedom, but the faculty cannot be renounced. Thus the Vincentians who enjoy the privilege of blessing the Miraculous Medal cannot individually renounce their faculty to enrich these medals. Nor can individual Franciscans renounce their power to bless the cord of Saint Francis.

The practice of the Church from the days of the early Popes was to urge the conservation of the privileges accorded to Bishoprics, and dignities of all kinds. These privileges can be considered in relation to the dignity itself, such as an ancient See, or Patriarchate, or in relation to the occupant of the See, as for instance, the Bishop of Ostia, or the Patriarch of Venice.

---

46 Slater, *o.c.*, v. I, p. 129.

Gratian[47] devotes over twenty canons to decrees emanating from the Roman See in regard to the privileges pertaining to the Bishoprics. After the manner of an example showing the solicitude of Rome that privileges be kept intact, one or the other of the more noteworthy canons can well be quoted. The exact term *renuntiare* is not found in any of these canons, but from the care and tenacity enjoined on the occupants of the privileged Sees, it can be argued that they were not free to renounce their privileges. Saint Hormisdas wrote thus: *Servatis privilegiis metropolitanorum vices vobis apostolicae sedis delegamus, ut inspectis istis, sive ea, quae a nobis sunt nuper mandata, serventur, sive quae de ecclesiasticis causis tuae revelationi contigerit, sub tua nobis insinuatione pandantur. Erit hoc studii ac sollicitudinis tuae, ut talem te in his, quae iniunguntur, exhibeas, ut fidem integritatemque eius, cuius curam suscipis, imiteris.*[48] Saint Gregory likewise emphasizes his own regard for the preservation of privileges. The Pope wrote thus to Dominic, Bishop of Carthage: *De ecclesiasticis privilegiis quod vestra fraternitas scribit, hoc postposita dubitatione teneat, quia sicut nostra defendimus, ita singulis quibusque ecclesiis sua iura servamus, nec cuilibet gratia favente ultra quam meretur impertior, nec ulli hoc, quod sui iuris est, ambitu stimulante derogabo: sed fratres meos per omnia honorare cupio, sicut honore singulos subvehi, dummodo non sit quod alteri iure ab altero possit opponi.*[49]

Commonly personal privileges, likewise, are not subject to private renunciation. These commonly personal privileges accrue to the occupants of a dignity, *e. g.*, the office of a Bishop, and are conceded to an individual person by reason of the office he holds. Personal merit, and ability are not the direct motives for conceding such

[47] C. 1-23, C. XXV, q. 2.
[48] C. 6, C. XXV, q. 2.
[49] C. 7, C. XXV, q. 2.

privileges. Therefore, since the beneficiary himself is not the entire final cause of commonly personal privileges, he cannot renounce his rights.

A private person is also incompetent to renounce the privileges attached to a place. The word "place" includes sanctuaries, shrines, and, in fact, any place which can be the subject of privilege. Frequently the tomb of a saint, or a miraculous picture of Our Lady will be enriched with some special privileges, such as a votive mass on otherwise forbidden days. Such privileges are not under the dominion of the caretaker of the shrine, or sanctuary. For instance, the Portiuncula chapel in Assisi enjoys the privilege of having a votive mass of the Blessed Virgin celebrated there every day in the year except three or four high festivals. Similarly, at the shrine of Our Lady of Perpetual Help in Rome, the votive mass can be said very frequently during the year. Instances like these could be recounted over several pages, even if consideration were merely confined to Italian sanctuaries. In some of these sacred places an Order, or a Congregation is in charge, in others secular priests watch over the venerable places. Neither the one nor the other can renounce the privileges attached to the shrine. The reason for this is not far to seek: in order to renounce a privilege, the first requisite is that the privilege be a personal right over which one has control. In the case of sacred places, the use at most of the privilege is conceded to the caretaker.[50] Should he be removed, the use of the privilege passes to his successor.

The Code, therefore, is explicit in denying to private persons the capacity of renouncing privileges grant-

---

50 Frequently not even the full use of the privilege is granted to the caretakers of shrines. For instance, at the shrine of Our Lady of Perpetual Help, the resident Redemptorists are allowed to celebrate the special votive mass but once a month, while visiting priests can celebrate this mass on almost every double feast.

ed to a community, dignity, or place. But can a community itself renounce a privilege? It is clear that a dignity, or a place cannot renounce its privileges since it is a non-collegiate moral person. A collegiate moral person, however, such as a religious community has an active voice in regard to its fortunes. The Code does not expressly concede renunciation of privileges to a community. Yet in denying renunciation in certain instances, the Code implies the faculty of renunciation in non-prohibited cases.

In the old law, Reiffenstuel[51] maintained that a moral person could renounce its privileges. This eminent canonist based his conclusion on decisions of Pope Innocent III.[52] Since the publication of the Code, Blat[53] deduces this faculty from a comparison of paragraphs 3 and 4 of canon 72. Indeed it would be difficult to see how renunciation could be conceded to an individual person and denied to a community, or assembly acting as a unit.[54] It is understood, of course, that the privilege is one of the proper sense of the word, entirely excluding favorable laws. Positive legislation may limit the exercise of renunciation because of possible loss to a third party, or prejudice of other rights. Canon 72 does, in fact, thus limit renunciation of privileges.

There are two instances when a community, or an assembly cannot renounce its privileges. The first instances concern the privileges granted by law. Particular law is meant here. Arguing from the prohibition enjoined on renunciation of privileges granted in common law, the reason for the incompetency of the community in the case at hand becomes evident. Particular law differs widely from particular concession. All the

---

51 Reiffenstuel, *o.c.*, lib. V, tit. XXXIII, n. 195.

52 C. 8, X, *de constitutionibus*, I, 2; c. 22, X, *de praebendis et dignitatibus*, III, 5.

53 Blat, *o.c.*, v. I, n. 140.

54 Maroto, *o.c.*, v. 1, n. 301.

elements of a law are found proportionately in the former, while some of the essential notes of a law are lacking in the latter. That a particular law should grant a privilege, does not destroy its juridical character. Hence if it were possible to renounce the privilege thus obtained from particular law, renunciation of the law itself would be involved. Therefore, the subject of a privilege cannot renounce the favor which constitutes the particular law.

Let this reasoning be applied to a concrete case. The Code prescribes a definite form of election.[55] An Order, however, may have a different and perhaps simpler form prescribed in its constitutions. The Holy See approves the constitutions thereby making them law for the community. In this case the Order is not permitted to renounce the form of election approved in the Rule. Other instances are found in particular prescriptions in approved constitutions concerning terms of office, age of Superiors, officials, etc.

The second case in which renunciation of privileges is denied to a community, or an assembly occurs when such renunciation would entail prejudice to the rights of the Church, or some other third party. In this instance the question of particular law does not enter. Consideration is confined to privileges in the strict sense of the word. The restriction placed on renunciation here is derived from the necessity of protecting the rights of interested parties.[56] No third person should suffer because a community chooses to divest itself of a privilege. Thus, two distinct communities may have obtained the privilege of soliciting alms. One of these communities finds that it does not need this support and decides to renounce its privilege. If it should do so a direct, or at least an indirect loss may be suffered by the second

55 Can. 161-178.
56 Reiffenstuel, *o.c.*, lib. V, tit. XXXIII, n. 196.

community, either by positive pressure brought to bear upon it to renounce its privilege, or by loss sustained because former contributors may think that it too has renounced its privilege. Distinctions will not always be made between community and community, and if one no longer solicits alms, contributors may well think that the other has acted similarly, thus entailing diminution of necessary support. If this loss be considerable, the now self-supporting community cannot renounce its privilege. Interested parties, however, for whose benefit such renunciation is forbidden need not be communities, or moral persons. Any one at all who will suffer considerably has rights which must be protected.

### 3. *Loss of Privileges by reason of the Grantor's loss of Power.*

**Can. 73. Resoluto iure concedentis, privilegia non exstinguuntur, nisi data fuerint cum clausula: ad beneplacitum nostrum, vel alia aequipollenti.**

Privileges granted by a Superior are usually not affected by his subsequent loss of power. This loss of authority may result from transfer, resignation, removal or death. Whatever be the cause of the loss of jurisdiction, privileges granted under the Superior are unaffected unless the rescript, or verbal concession definitely provided that the privilege is to be affected by the fortunes of its author. The Code suggests the formula *ad beneplacitum nostrum.* A similar expression would be *quamdiu sum Superior,* or, *donec vixero.*

The formula *ad beneplacitum Sedis Apostolicae,* or, simply, *ad beneplacitum Sedis* would not be of the same force, because the Apostolic See does not cease with the death of the Holy Father.[57] Boniface VIII defines the issue clearly in one of his decretals: *Si gratiose tibi a*

---

[57] Barbosa, *o.c., De clausulis usufrequentioribus,* Claus. III, n. 5.

*Romano Pontifice concedatur, ut beneficia, quae tempore tuae promotionis obtinebas, posses usque ad suae voluntatis beneplacitum retinere: huiusmodi gratia per eius obitum, per quem ipsius beneplacitum omnino exstinguitur, eo ipso expirat. Secus autem, si usque ad apostolicae sedis beneplacitum gratia concedatur praedicta. Tunc enim, quia sedes ipsa non moritur, durabit perpetuo, nisi a successore fuerit revocata.*[58]

Canon 73 exemplifies the general principles governing the extinction of rescripts.[59] A review of the exercise of these principles will help to understand their application to privileges.

Lucius III, in writing to the Archbishop of Canterbury and his Suffragans stated that a Papal rescript did not cease with the death of the Pope, provided litigation had begun.[60] A decision of Boniface VIII approaches more closely to the matter of privileges: *Si super gratia, cuiquam ab apostolica sede facta, exsecutores fuerint deputati, aequum esse censemus, ut, sicut ipsa gratia, licet non sit in eius exsecutione processum, morte non perimitur concedentis, sic nec etiam re integra perimatur exsecutoribus data potestas, quam, veluti gratiae praedictae accessoriam, naturam sequi congruit principalis; ne gratiam eandem vel reddi quandocumque omnino inutilem, vel ipsius effectum in tempus longius cum illius dispendio, cui facta existit, differri contingat.*[61] Another decision of the same Pontiff concerns a privilege granted by the Holy See to select a worthy beneficiary in a certain church. The restriction of the concession is expressly stated in the text. *Huiusmodi concessio, quam, quum specialem gratiam contineat, decet esse mansuram, non expirat etiam re integra per obitum concedentis. Secus, si super provisione certae personae facienda sit*

58 C. 5, *de rescriptis*, I, 3 in VI.
59 Can. 61.
60 C. 19, X, *de officio et potestate iudicis delegati*, I, 29.
61 C. 9, *de officio et potestate iudicis delegati*, I, 14 in VI.

*data potestas eidem non ob suam, sed eius, cui provideri mandatur, gratiam vel favorem; illa quidem exspirat omnino, si concedens re integra moriatur.*[62]

It is hardly necessary to state that the clause *ad beneplacitum meum,* or its equivalent must be evident. This clause is never presumed.[63]

### 4. *Loss of Personal Privileges.*

**Can. 74. Privilegium personale personam sequitur et cum ipsa exstinguitur.**

Canon 74 distinguishes between the use and the extinction of personal privileges. The use of personal privileges was already seen in the chapter on the use of privileges.[64] Attention at present will be confined to the loss of personal privileges.

The personal privilege meant in canon 74 is of the class known as *individually personal* privileges. Such privileges are attached to the physical person of the grantee. They are conceded as a favor to the individual himself without any reference at all to the office, or dignity which he might hold. Hence the reason for the concession of such privileges ceases with the death of the grantee, and does not pass to his heirs, or successors.

A personal privilege which a grantee may possess in common with other beneficiaries also ceases with the death of the grantee, provided the matter of the privilege is divisible. But should the privilege be conceded rather to an association, the privilege would not cease with the extinction of one of the grantees.

Privileges accruing to physical persons by reason of their state, office, or dignity are not considered strictly personal privileges in the sense that they cease with the

---

62 C. 36, *de praebendis et dignitatibus,* III, 4 in VI.
63 R.J. 15 in VI.
64 Cf. p. 87, *et seq.*

death of the physical person, or grantee. Commonly personal privileges, then, such as the privileges of Cardinals and Bishops do not cease with the death of the Prelate. These privileges, however, must be considered personal at least in the sense that their use is legitimate wherever the grantee happens to be. The privilege of blessing rosaries, for instance,[65] can be used lawfully in any place.

### 5. *Loss of Real Privileges.*

**Can. 75. Privilegia realia cessant per absolutum rei vel loci interitum; privilegia vero localia, si locus intra quinquaginta annos restituatur, reviviscunt.**

Altho the formal aspect of a real privilege has already[66] been explained, it is well to recall its relation to the physical beneficiary who enjoys its rights. A physical person may enjoy a privilege granted in his own name, or he may enjoy a privilege by reason of his office, or in a general way, by reason of his connection with a dignity, place, community or assembly. In the latter instances the privilege adheres to the dignity, etc., while its use, and benefit accrues to the occupant of the dignity, etc. Such a privilege is called a real privilege (from Lt., *res*). This *res* can be anything which is not a physical ecclesiastical person:[67] hence, sacred objects, places, dignities, offices, assemblies, communities, etc.

Real privileges are lost by the absolute destruction of the thing or place. This principle offers no difficulties except for the correct interpretation of the word "absolute." A thing, *e. g.*, a sacred image, church, can be said to be absolutely destroyed when it is substantially destroyed. A place can be considered in the same light. Hence it is not necessary in every case that the thing

65 Can. 239, § 1, n. 5 for Cardinals; can. 349, § 1, n. 1 for Bishops.

66 Cf. p. 31.

67 Cicognani, *o.c.*, p. 304.

or place be so completely obliterated that scarcely any trace of its former existence remains. The other extreme must likewise be avoided. Therefore, the partial destruction which would demand the reconstruction of a church would not yet deprive the church of its privileges.

It is worth while remarking here, with Blat[68] and Cicognani,[69] that the unsuitability of a place in regard to its first purpose does not cause a loss of its privileges. Thus, owing to some calamity, a church may be roofless, or without a sanctuary. Holy Mass, perhaps, could not well be celebrated in such a church for reasons of respect for the August Sacrifice, or because of possible danger to life. No matter how long this condition remains, the church's privileges would be intact. Its destruction is not absolute.

The absolute destruction of a thing will in many cases depend upon its nature. Actual physical destruction can occur to sacred objects, such as statues, crosses, etc. Their privileges cease with the destruction of the thing. Sale of these articles will also cause a loss of indulgences.[70] Dignities and offices can be suppressed by proper authority. When this happens, the privileges cease.[71] Assemblies which are not juridical moral persons can be dissolved. Their privileges are lost at dissolution. Communities, however, and all moral persons can be suppressed by legitimate authority, or cease by the defection or death of its members. If the moral person is suppressed its privileges cease at once, but if death, or defection from membership intervenes, the moral person is juridically considered to exist for another hundred years,[72] and therefore its privileges con-

68 Blat, *o.c.*, v. I, n. 143.
69 Cicognani, *o.c.*, p. 304-5.
70 Can. 924, § 2.
71 Ayrinhac, *o.c.*, n. 165.
72 Can. 102, § 1.

tinue for that length of time. According to canon 102, § 2 as long as one member of the moral person lives, all the rights of the association accrue to him.

As far as the principle of cessation is concerned, the absolute destruction of a thing terminates its privileges. But the Code makes an exception for real privileges attached to a place. These are the so-called local privileges. The restitution of a local privilege is called *reviviscentia.* This restitution of local privileges comes from the fact of rebuilding the place, and is not due to a new concession of privileges.

Formerly there was no definite time during which local privileges could be revived. As long as there was hope of rebuilding a place its privileges were not irretrievably lost. Now, however, a period of fifty years is allowed before local privileges finally lapse. Since the fifty years' grace will scarcely begin with the horological computation of the day, the first day of destruction is not counted and the time expires with the end of the last day of the time-allowance.

An application of the exception in favor local privileges is found in canon 924, § 1. Indulgences which were attached to a church revive, if the church is rebuilt within fifty years. This is true even if the church had been totally destroyed, as may happen by earthquake, or fire. Besides the condition of time, two other conditions must be fulfilled: first, the church must be rebuilt in the same place, or in nearly the same place where the destroyed church stood, and second, the church must be rebuilt under the same title.[73] Non-fulfillment of these conditions will cause the privileges of the church to cease entirely.

---

73 Can. 924, § 1. *Ad norman can 75, indulgentiae adnexae alicui ecclesiae non cessant, si ecclesia funditus evertatur rursusque intra quinquaginta annos aedificetur in eodem vel fere eodem loco et sub eodem titulo.*

An understanding of the provisions of canons 75 and 924 will be valuable to a priest, or a community who may take over a ruined church and attempt to rebuild it. Often enough in times of war, and otherwise unsettled conditions a community or secular priest may be driven from his church and the building destroyed. The same resident community or priest may never return, but the ruined church might be rebuilt under different auspices. If the list of privileges were preserved, and the accurate date of the church's destruction known, the matter of privileges would be greatly simplified, many doubts and scruples avoided, and beneficent indulgences gained. The privileges, however, which belonged to the community itself would not be regained unless the same community returned.[74]

### 6. *Loss of Privileges by Non-use, or by Contrary Use of a Privilege.*

**Can. 76. Per non usum vel per usum contrarium privilegia aliis haud onerosa non cessant; quae vero in aliorum gravamen cedunt, amittuntur, si accedat legitima praescriptio vel tacita renuntiatio.**

Canon 76 distinguishes between privileges which do not curtail the rights of interested parties, and privileges which cause some diminution of these rights. The former class of privileges do not cease by non-use, or even by contrary use, while the latter are lost by prescription, or by tacit renunciation.

*Non-use* of a privilege is the free selection to omit exercising the right conceded by the privilege. All violence, or force of any kind must be excluded from any influence on the grantee's action. He must be free to exercise his right if he cares to do so. If the grantee should be forced to omit, or to forego his rights, the

[74] ASS. v. I, p. 239.

material act would indeed be non-use of a privilege, but the formal and determining character of the act would be lacking. This freedom from coaction is alike necessary in both classes of privilege distinguished in canon 76, but only in the second part of the canon does it bear any direct relation to the retention, or loss of a privilege. Since non-onerous privileges are not lost by non-use, it would be of no importance to stress the necessity of freedom of action.

*Contrary use* means that the person who enjoys a right by means of a privilege chooses to do the opposite. Contrary use is more than mere non-use of a privilege. The latter is in a sense negative, while the former requires a positive act opposed to the provisions of the privilege. Thus, for instance, a family may enjoy the privilege of a private oratory. Holy Mass, then can be celebrated in the oratory according to the stipulations of the rescript. Usually, high festivals will be excluded from the days on which Mass is allowed in such an oratory, but this is a detail which will not affect the matter at hand. Now, understanding the provisions of the privilege, the family elects to attend Mass at the parish church. If this happens consistently, the family is presumed to be acting contrary to its privilege. For the sake of illustration, all excuses are excluded, such as inability to secure a priest, special solemnity at the parish church, etc. Freedom of action, spoken of in regard to non-use of a privilege is equally applicable here. A person forced to forego his rights, and perform some opposite action cannot be said to act in a formal way contrary to his privilege.

With all this in mind, canon 76 can be examined. A word or two will suffice for the first part of this canon. Non-onerous privileges do not entail loss of rights, or increased duties on the part of a third person, and consequently, this third person's status is in no way affected by the non-use, or contrary use of a privilege. In such circumstances there would be little reason to penalize a grantee if he did not care to use his privilege. Non-onerous privileges, such as celebrating Mass on a portable altar, or gaining special indulgences, come under this head and would not cease by non-use, or contrary use.

The second part of canon 76 stipulates how onerous privileges are lost. Occasional non-use, or contrary use of these privileges does not argue their loss. Even protracted omission, extending over the period of some months, does not cause the loss of these privileges. Since the Code opposes prescription to non-use, and tacit renunciation to contrary use, it will be best to consider the items separately.

*Prescription* is the acquisition of rights, or the liberation from burdens by means of the transfer of rights, or the cancellation of burdens. Prescription supposes a just title, possession, and a definite period of time.[75] In the matter at hand, prescription is limited to the rights conceded by a privilege. From these rights release is sought by a third party. Such prescription is called liberative prescription. The time required for liberative prescription is the same as is necessary to acquire a privilege by prescription. Therefore thirty years of non-use of a privilege by a moral person will cause its loss by liberative prescription.[76]

*Tacit renunciation* is present when a privileged person can use the favor granted him but elects to do something else. His intention to renounce his privilege is gathered from the protracted contrary use of the privilege he possesses. Acting in accordance with this presumed intention, the legislator reduces the relation between the privileged person and interested parties to

---

75 Cf. pp. 65-66.
76 C. 1511; cf. Cicognani, *o.c.*, p. 307.

the requirements of law.[77] The same time is required for liberation by tacit renunciation as is necessary for release by means of prescription. It is important, however, to remember that the grantee must be capable of renouncing his privilege. He cannot, even tacitly, renounce a privilege which is not entirely his own.

### 7. *Loss of Privileges because of altered Circumstances; lapse of time; and exhaustion of the number of Cases.*

**Can. 77. Cessat quoque privilegium, si temporis progressu rerum adiuncta sic, iudicio Superioris, immutentur ut noxium evaserit, aut eius usus illicitus fiat; item elapso tempore vel expleto numero casuum pro quibus privilegium fuit concessum, firmo praescripto can. 207, § 2.**

Circumstances, not existing at the time when the privilege was conceded, can often so change the beneficial aspect of a privilege so as to render it seriously harmful.[78] To allow the use of a privilege under such untoward circumstances would be legally wrong.[79] A moral obligation to revoke or cancel the privilege would also exist, but this question is foreign to the present study.

The legal aspect of the case ought to be emphasized. An example from the Decretals will set the matter in its proper light.

A privilege of not contributing tithes had been granted to some monasteries long before the days of Pope Alexander III. The condition of the monasteries at the time of the concession of the privilege was such that no scandal would arise if they were exempted from legitimate tribute. With spread of monasticism, and with the broad lands bequeathed to deserving monas-

77 Cicognani, *o.c.*, l.c.
78 Raus, *o.c.*, n. 40, IV.
79 Ballerini-Palmieri, *o.c.*, v. I, n. 392.

teries by friends, the continued use of the privilege *non solvendi decimas* became a serious burden on some other houses of monks. Naturally it was only a question of time before the matter came to the attention of the Pope. Alexander III writes that many complaints had come to him on this head, and as a consequence he urged a compromise so that justice might be served on all sides, and the good name of the monks preserved: *Quia vero non decet honestatem sive religionem monasticam litibus et contentionibus intendere, Discretioni vestrae per apostolica scripta mandamus, consulimus, et hortamur, quatenus cum praedicto abbate et fratribus super ipsis decimis et aliis, unde inter vos est controversia, pacifice componatis, ne pro huiusmodi contentionibus fama vestrae religionis valeat denigrari.*[80]

Rule 61 of Sexto Bonifacii VIII is applicable here: *Quod ob gratiam alicuius conceditur non est in eius dispendium retorquendum.*

Besides rendering a privilege directly harmful, a change of circumstances may make the use of the privilege illicit. This may happen without any abuse of the privilege and be due to circumstances over which the grantee has no control. The reason for the loss of the privilege in this case is evident. The Superior clearly could not concede a privilege under such unlawful conditions.

The judgments of men vary, and what seems harmful, or unlawful to one may not be so to another. Hence the wise provision of the Code in determining who is the judge in this matter. The Superior of the grantee is the sole judge. Consequently, his judgment must be followed, no matter what interested parties may think of the justice of his decision. However, a Superior should consider the character of the individual privilege. Odious privileges necessarily entail some injury to the rights

80 C. 9, X, *de decimis, primitiis et oblationibus*, III, 30.

of others. This element was already considered when the privilege was granted. Allegation of no more injury than this can scarcely demand the cancellation of a privilege.

The second part of canon 77 is so clear that comment is unnecessary. But it might be said that these provisions concerning lapse of time, and completion of cases, refer primarily to the habitual faculties considered in canon 66.

An extension of the faculties conceded for the internal forum is granted in canon 207, § 2. The condition stated there must be fulfilled. Not every act beyond the time or case limit is valid but only those which occur thru inadvertence. Hence, if an Ordinary or his delegate inadvertently went beyond these limits of his faculties, thinking he had a longer time, or a larger number of cases, his acts would be valid. The case would not be the same if an Ordinary, realizing that his faculties had expired, nevertheless acted because of an oversight in not requesting renewal of his faculties in seasonable time. But in some instances, canon 81 could be invoked and the acts thereby rendered valid.[81]

### 8. *Abuse of a Privilege.*

**Can. 78. Qui abutitur potestate sibi ex privilegio permissa, privilegio ipso privari meretur; et Ordinarius Sanctam Sedem monere ne omittat, si quis privilegio ab eadem concesso graviter abutatur.**

Properly speaking, an exposition of possible abuses of privileges has no place in a chapter on the loss of this place.

81 Can. 81. *A generalibus Ecclesiae legibus Ordinarii infra Romanum Pontificem dispensare nequeunt, ne in casu quidem peculiari, nisi haec potestas eisdem fuerit explicite vel implicite concessa, aut nisi difficilis sit recursus ad Sanctam Sedem et simul in mora sit periculum gravis damni, et de dispensatione agatur quae a Sede Apostolica concedi solet.*

privileges. However, there is a connection of cause and usual effect which justifies the treatment of canon 78 in

Gratian relates a classical example of an abuse of a privilege. The Bishop of Ravenna enjoyed the privilege of consecrating Bishops. But by an abuse which Pope Gregory called "*amentia*" the Bishop consecrated an unwilling cleric. The decree recorded by Gratian on this incident almost supplies the initial words of canon 78. The penalty in this case was not drastic, but no doubt was left in the mind of the offending Prelate what would happen if the deed were repeated.[82]

Passing from the principle to be followed as enunciated in Gratian's collection of decrees, one finds concrete examples of condign punishment meted out to those who abused the rights granted to them by a privilege. Gregory IX in his letter to the Bishop of Paris enumerates abuses which entail the loss of privileges.[83] Innocent III deprived the canons of Siena of the privilege of election.[84] The same Pontiff tempered the privilege of obtaining the revenues from non-resident benefices. This privilege had been conceded to some students who could not reside at the place of their benefices and at the same time continue their studies. In order to foster study, the onus of residence was alleviated. But instead of using their time for study, a number of the students enjoyed a vacation at a villa, or at some other place less conducive to study. The Pope ruled that this was an abuse of the privilege and consequently decreed that the revenues of the benefices would not accrue to the absentees.[85] Another case decided by Innocent III concerned the abuse of a privilege which did not allow a transfer

82 C. 7, D. LXXIV. *Denunciamus autem, quod, si post haec aliquid tale presumpseris, et aliquem seu episcopum, vel presbiterum, vel diaconum invitum facere forte crederis, ordinationes tibi Ravennatis ecclesiae vel Emiliensis noveris auferendas.*

83 C. 43, X, *de rescriptis*, I, 3.

84 C. 2, X, *de postulatione praelatorum*, I, 5.

85 C. 12, X, *de clericis non residentibus in ecclesia vel praebenda*, III, 4.

from one religious Order to another. The abuse of the privilege consisted in denying transfer to a stricter Order when the religious, actuated by pure motives, wished to lead a more mortified life. In this instance the Pope did not revoke the privilege but plainly stated the limits within which it would have to be used, recalling to the mind of the offending Superiors *privilegium meretur amittere qui sibi concessa abutitur potestate.*[86]

The abuse in these cases, as in others, consisted in acting beyond the legitimate provisions of a privilege.[87] If it be remembered what a privilege is, and how the very concession of a privilege depends on the will of a Superior, it will readily be seen what a travesty of justice is involved in an abuse of a privilege. Yet despite this injustice, abuse of itself does not cancel a privilege for the reason that an express, or tacit act of the Superior is necessary to obtain this end. Occasionally, too, an abuse may result from a misunderstanding of the terms of a privilege with little or no bad will at all attached to the action. In such a case it is fitting that a Superior decide the extent and possible malice of the abuse.

In order to correct the abuse of a privilege, it is necessary that the proper Superior become acquainted with the abuse. If the abuse occurs within the Superior's immediate vision, he can take suitable action at once. But often enough abuses will occur in such a way that the proper Superior will remain in ignorance of them. Hence, in the matter of Papal privileges, the Code demands that Ordinaries advise the Holy See of abuses of privileges. All Superiors who come under the name "Ordinary"[88] are included.

The denunication is to be made to the Holy See both when the abuse is connected with a personal privi-

---

86 C. 18, X, *de regularibus et transeuntibus ad religionem*, III, 31.
87 Zoesius, *o.c.*, lib. V, tit. XXXIII, n. 38.
88 Can. 198, § 1.

lege and when the community itself is at fault. Abuses of local privileges must likewise be reported.

There is a word in canon 78 which argues for prudence. A privilege must be abused *graviter* before the offense ought to be reported to the Holy See. Hence some slight excess would not call for vigorous action. Of course, what is to constitute a serious abuse must be left to the judgment of the Ordinary who detects it. Once the report has been made, the Holy See will weigh the matter justly and act accordingly.

## CHAPTER VIII

## PROOF OF A PRIVILEGE.

**Canon 79. Quamvis privilegia, oretenus a Sancta Sede obtenta, ipsi petenti in foro conscientiae suffragentur, nemo tamen potest cuiusvis privilegii usum adversus quemquam in foro externo vindicare nisi privilegium ipsum sibi concessum esse legitime evincat.**

The element of proof does not touch the nature of a privilege. It is one thing to enjoy the possession of a favor, and quite another to defend it with a proper document, or a sufficient number of witnesses. It should not be said that the lack of documentary evidence, or the absence of witnesses, precludes all use of a privilege. Many cases can and will arise when such proof would not be necessary.

Canon 79 says that verbal privileges, granted by the Holy See, are of value in the forum of conscience. This means that such privileges can be used without scruple as long as their use does not extend beyond the limits of this forum. It matters little whether the concessions be temporary, or perpetual.[1]

There is no intrinsic difference in the value of verbal and written privileges.[2] Whatever practical utility a document may bring to a privilege, or whatever testi-

---

1 *The Ordo Servandus, published by the Cardinal Secretary of State, contained practically the same words as Canon 79. Gratiae, quas quis pro se a Sancta Sede oretenus assequitur, ipsi petenti in foro conscientiae suffragantur. Nemo tamen potest cuiuscumque privilegii usum adversus quemquam vindicare, nisi privilegium ipsum legitime probet. Ordo servandus in S. Congregationibus, Tribunalibus, Officiis Romanae Curiae,* 29 *Sept.*, 1908, *Pars II, Normae peculiares, cap. III, n.* 2, *in Martin, o.c., p.* 364. *The Code in adding in foro externo, limits the necessity of proof to the external forum only.*

2 Reiffenstuel, *o.c.*, lib. V, tit. XXXIII, no. 150.

mony approved witnesses may offer in support of a privilege, the advantage derived does not affect the essential characteristics of a privilege. This follows as a logical consequence of the non-necessity of writing in the concession of a privilege.

In the external forum, however, it is necessary to prove a privilege in order to defend its use.[3] Since the external forum may be either judicial or extra-judicial, proof of a privilege is required for both. It is clear enough that proof should be of necessity in the matter of a trial so that a proper judgment may be rendered. But Innocent X went beyond this. In his constitution, *Cum sicut,* May 14, 1648, he demanded proof of privileges also in an extra-judicial matter. The question was proposed thus: *An privilegia, quae conceduntur contra jurisdictionem Ordinarii et quibus gaudent, et gaudere praetendunt Regulares praedicti* (missionaries in India) *debeant Episcopis notificari, sive insinuari?* The answer given by Pope Innocent was: *Regulares teneri hujusmodi privilegia Episcopo exhibere, si eis uti voluerint.*[4] This was only a particular case and, it might be objected, one in which an Episcopal power was infringed, and hence could not be adduced as a principle to govern all cases. Yet if it be observed that the answer of Pope Innocent is nothing more than a rational statement made to prevent indiscrimate and unrestrained assertions of privilege by which rights of interested parties might be wantonly abused, it will be seen that the Pope is merely applying a principle of justice and prudence rather than excogitating a rule to fit an individual case.

The Decretals are not lacking in examples which imply the same necessity of legitimate proof of privilege. In the time of Alexander III some churches paid an annual tribute to the Holy See. Some thought that this

[3] Craisson, *o.c.,* v. I, n. 163; Makee, *o.c.,* v. I, n. 316,

[4] Fontes, n. 232.

tribute gave them the privilege of exemption from the jurisdiction of the diocesan Bishop. The Pope admitted that this privilege might have been granted, but it did not follow as a necessary consequence from the donation made to the Holy See. Therefore: *Inspicienda sunt ergo ipsarum ecclesiarum privilegia, et ipsorum tenor est diligentius attendendus, ut, si fuerit deprehensum, quod ecclesia, quae censum solvit, specialiter B. Petri iuris existat, et ad indicium perceptae libertatis census annuus conferatur, non immerito poterit speciali praerogativa gaudere. Si vero ad indicium perceptae protectionis census persolvitur, non ex hoc iuri diocesani episcopi aliquid videtur esse subtractum.*[5]

Boniface VIII stresses the same necessity of proof of privilege. Without mincing words, and stating his reasons clearly, the Pontiff writes: *Quum personae ecclesiasticae tam religiosae quam saeculares plura praesumant, quae ipsis infamiam pariunt, et aliis inferunt laesionem, praetextu exemptionis vel libertatis, quam asserunt se habere, ordinariorum correctiones et ordinationes subterfugientes, ac eorum forum sive iudicium declinantes: nos, volentes super hoc de salubri remedio providere, statuimus, ut hi, qui asserunt per privilegia seu indulgentias apostolicae sedis exemptos, a locorum ordinariis requisiti huiusmodi privilegia vel indulgentias, quibus se dicunt fore munitos, ipsis ordinariis in loco congruo et securo, aut aliquibus prudentibus viris omni suspicione carentibus, ad hoc per dictos ordinarios deputatis, infra terminum competentem, pro facti qualitate ipsorum ordinariorum vel delegatorum suorum arbitrio moderandum, iusto impedimento cessante ostendere, ac ad legendum integraliter exhibere, nec non de articulis, de quibus controversia fuerit, transcriptum tradere teneantur.*[6]

---

5 C. 8, X, *de privilegiis et excessibus privilegiatorum*, V, 33.
6 C. 7, *de privilegiis et excessibus privilegiatorum*, V, 7, in VI.

Cocchi[7] mentions three ways in which, ordinarily, the existence of a privilege may be proved. *Witnesses* can attest the concession of a privilege provided they are above suspicion. Two witnesses at least are required, especially in judicial matters,[8] since one witness ordinarily does not supply sufficient proof.[9]

Canons 1789-1791 give indications of how the faith of witnesses is to be tested. Altho these canons primarily refer to judicial processes, the suggestions offered might well be followed in weighing evidence procured in extrajudicial matter.[10]

*Prescription* is the second method of proving a privilege mentioned by Cocchi. All the requisites described and explained in a former chapter[11] will have to be consulted.

The third method of proving a privilege is by *document.* This is the most satisfactory method. Possible suspicion of collusion in the case of witnesses, or possible bad faith unable to be detected in the case of prescription, hardly have any occasion to occur in the case of a document. The document must, of course, be duly authenticated. If there should be question of authenticating an original oral grant, the Code prescribes who can act in this matter, but if the question should concern an exem-

---

7 Cocchi, *o.c.*, v. I, n. 123.

8 C. 23, 47, X, *de privilegiis et excessibus privilegiatorum*, V, 33.

9 C. 1791, § 1. Cf. Noval, *o.c.*, n. 512; Sebastianelli, *o.c.*, n. 150; Zoesius, *o.c.*, lib. V, tit. XXXIII, n. 4.

10 Since Canon 1789 supplies a good criterion of the worth of a witness, it is well to quote the canon in full. *In aestimandis testimoniis judex prae oculis habeat:* 1. *Quae conditio sit personae, quaeve honestas et an aliqua dignitate testis praefulgeat;* 2. *Utrum de scientia propria, praesertim de visu et auditu proprio testificetur, an de credulitate, de fama, aut de auditu ab aliis;* 3. *Utrum testis constans sit et firmiter sibi cohaereat; an varius, incertus, vel vacillans;* 4. *Denique utrum testimonii contestes habeat, an sit singularis.* Cf. Noval, *o.c.*, n. 510; Lega, *o.c.*, v. I, n. 490; Sebastianelli, *o.c.*, n. 142, 148, 149.

11 See chapter IV, p. 64, *et seq.*

plar of the original document, any canonical notary can attest it.

Cardinals, by virtue of their privilege,[12] can authenticate a document, testifying to a privilege granted by the Holy Father *vivae vocis oraculo.* The testimony of one Cardinal suffices. Secretaries of the Roman Congregations are similarly competent in affairs of their own congregation.

*Presumption* can also serve to prove a privilege, especially if the presumption is legal according to Canon 63, § 2. Such presumption cannot be attacked by mere denial. Unless the foundation of the presumption is dissolved, the law demands that the disputed privilege be accepted as legitimately conceded.[13]

---

12 C. 239, § 1, n. 17.

13 *Possessio centenaria vel immemorabilis inducit praesumptionem concessi privilegii.*

## CHAPTER IX

## FACULTIES.

Before attempting an exposition of Canon 66, which deals with habitual faculties, it will be well to set down a few introductory thoughts connected with faculties in general.

The English word "faculty" is evidently derived from the Latin "*facultas.*" The latter term, retaining some resemblance to the old Latin spelling (*facule-facile*), is in turn based upon the word "*facilitas.*" There is a difference between the two Latin words which is apparent without any examination. "*Facultas*" signifies a power, while "*facilitas*" denotes the ease with which a power can be exercised.

A faculty, then, etymologically, means a power, or a capacity to perform some action. The scope of this action cannot be found in the root-meaning of the word "faculty."

The exact time when the word "faculty" came to have a definite meaning in Canon law can scarcely be assigned with any degree of accuracy. In 1622, when the Congregation for the Propagation of the Faith was instituted, the term "faculty" had already found its way into canon Law. In its very first session, January 14, 1622, the Congregation proposed to issue a Bull announcing the erection of the Congregation *cum suis facultatibus et privilegiis.*[1] Missionary work, which the new Congregation was to supervise, had already existed for some time, and it would be well within reason to suppose that faculties were granted as soon as the real need for them arose in missionary fields. Add to this the labors

[1] Coll. n. 1.

of Bishops and priests in Europe to bring back to the Church those who had fallen since the first signs of Luther's rebellion and the origin of faculties may be sought a century earlier than 1622.

That the concession of faculties demanded the greatest prudence is evident from the careful consideration accompanying the construction of the new formulas of 1637.[2] A middle path had to be followed between severity and laxity. In this document of 1637 the words *"facultas"* and *"formula"* are used without any further attempt to clarify their meaning.

In the same year, 1637, the Congregation of the Propaganda, realizing the insufficiency of the formulas then existing to meet the needs of missionaries, decided to settle upon some general rules to govern the concession of formulas containing faculties. These rules embodied consideration of the character of the people who were converted to the faith, their distance from the Holy See, the permission or prohibition to practice their faith, and, finally, the dignity and office of the grantee.[3] These general rules were to be supplemented according to individual needs.

Altho for obvious reasons, the greater number of faculties came in part directly from the Congregation of the Propaganda, yet it must not be supposed that other Congregations, and Tribunals of the Roman Curia did not possess similar powers in their own proper spheres. The Holy Office, for instance, conceded faculties in marriage cases, while the Sacred Penitentiary was competent in matters of the internal forum. Today, canons 247-263 give the competence of the various Congregations and Tribunals.

The similarity of a "faculty" to a "privilege" is so close that no proper definition seems to have been given

---

2 Coll. n. 88.
3 Coll. n. 87.

to the former before the appearance of Konings-Putzer's *Commentarium in Facultates Apostolicas.* In this work a faculty is defined as *Potestas, quam Superior ecclesiasticus jurisdictione in foro externo praeditus cuidam sibi aliquo modo subdito personaliter concedit, aliquid sive in foro conscientiae tantum sive etiam pro foro externo valide aut licite aut saltem tuto agendi.*[4] Since then (1893), in a general way, authors have followed this definition.[5]

However, an observation may be made with Motry concerning the propriety of limiting the concession of faculties to superiors who enjoy jurisdiction in the external forum.[6] Canon 258 limits the jurisdiction of the Sacred Penitentiary to the internum forum, both sacramental and non-sacramental. Absolutions, dispensations, etc., for this forum are granted by this Tribunal. Consequently, the Sacred Penitentiary is to be considered as the Superior for the internal forum even tho it has no jurisdiction in the external forum. In order, then, to include the concession of faculties granted by the Sacred Penitentiary, a change from *jurisdictione in foro externo praeditus* to *jurisdictione in foro respectivo praeditus* ought to be made in the definition of "faculty."

A more detailed analysis of the various definitions of "faculty" is beyond the scope of this study.[7] For the present purpose, the definition cited above with the correction in respect of Superiors will be found to accommodate all the grants known as faculties.[8]

There are three principal divisions of faculties. In respect of the object of the grant, faculties are (a) *jurisdictionales,* (b) *gratiae* or *licentiae,* (c) *ad caut-*

---

4 Konings-Putzer, *Commentarium in Facultates Apostolicas,* (*Neo-Eboraci,* 1893) n. 1.

5 E.g., Augustine, *o.c.,* p. 159-161; Maroto, *o.c.,* v. I, n. 294.

6 Motry, *Diocesan Faculties,* (Washington, 1922) p. 9-10.

7 Cf. Motry, *o.c.,* p. 7-19.

8 Motry, *o.c.,* p. 17.

*elam.*[9] The first class comprise the most important group of faculties because they supply the necessary validity of an act. The second class presupposes the validity of an act, but it grants permission to act. The third class may at times be real faculties, if the validity of an act would otherwise be wanting, but ordinarily faculties *ad cautelam* are conceded to remove doubt, or to quiet uneasy consciences.

In respect of duration, faculties may be *actual* or *habitual* according to the time, or number of cases for which the power is enjoyed. An *actual* faculty is limited to a single case. An *habitual* faculty is conceded for a certain length of time, or a definite number of cases.

In respect of the Superior who concedes the faculties, the grants are *Papal*, or *Episcopal.* It is scarcely necessary to state that Papal faculties may be granted personally by the Holy Father, or thru the competent Congregations or Tribunal. Episcopal faculties are granted by the Ordinary of the diocese. *Praelati Regulares* may also concede faculties.

The *general* and *particular extension* of faculties, as well as the *ordinary* and *extraordinary formulas* likewise supply a point of division according to which faculties may be considered.[10]

The interpretation of faculties follows the norms assigned to laws, rescripts, privileges, and clauses. This is the general principle which finds its application in regard to privileges in canon 67 of the Code. *Privilegium ex ipsius tenore aestimandum est, nec licet illud extendere aut restringere.* The rule cited by Wernz,[11] *facultates semper comprehensive, non extensive sunt interpretanda,* is still in the main applicable to faculties as

9 Wernz, *o.c.*, v. I, n. 163.

10 Wernz, *o.c.*, l.c.; Vermeersch has two appendices in which he gives the faculties conceded to Nuntii, etc., and Ordinaries of mission countries, v. I, n. 715-720.

11 Wernz, *o.c.*, v. I, n. 193.

they exist today. General terms will demand broad comprehensive interpretation, provided the meaning of the terms is not extended beyond their natural and legal sense.

Particular terms will receive a strict comprehensive interpretation.

The present practice of the Roman Curia will often help to solve doubts concerning the interpretation and use of faculties. This *"stylus"* (and *"praxis Curiae"*) consists of the rules derived from Papal constitutions, and from custom. According to these rules or norms the Curia conducts its work. Since the Roman Curia labors under the direct vigilance of the Pope, special importance is attached to the practice of his Curia. Diocesan Curias should presume that the Pope favors the same rules for them as he does for his own Curia. Apropos of this statement it is fitting to quote in full a question proposed to the Sacred Penitentiary: *An Episcopus, quando vi specialis indulti Apostolici in aliquo impedimento matrimonium dirimente dispensat, necessario et ad valorem dispensationis sequi debeat easdem illas regulas, quas in Curia Romana observant, ubi ipse Summus Pontifex in eodem impedimento iisdemque impedimenti gradibus dispensat?* The Tribunal answered, June 1, 1858, *Affirmative.*[12]

This response seems to refer to both the object of the dispensation and to the manner in which it is to be conceded. The Holy Office, however, tempered the answer to include the object only, provided the faculties did not require a precise method of concession.[13]

Faculties cease in the same way as other privileges. Revocation, renunciation, lapse of time, completion of cases, all have their application here. A word, however, may be added in regard to revocation of faculties. Often

---

[12] In Konings-Putzer, *o.c.*, n. 11.
[13] June 15, 1875, in Konings-Putzer, *o.c.*, n. 12.

enough the faculties which an Ordinary receives will be communicated to a priest of his diocese. Now if the Ordinary's faculties should be revoked, the priest would not thereby lose his faculties because he now possesses them in his own name.[14] But if the revocation should be general, the communicated faculties would also cease.

**Can. 66, § 1. Facultates habituales quae conceduntur vel in perpetuum vel ad praefinitum tempus aut certum numerum casuum, accensentur privilegiis praeter ius.**

The question of privileges beyond the law is not so easy a matter to understand as would be supposed from the description of such a privilege as offered, for instance, by Reiffenstuel. *Privilegium praeter ius* is granted *quando ipsamet materia, seu actus privilegii non est quidem in se iure prohibitus sed tamen non est nisi certis personis concessus.*[15] As an example of a privilege beyond the law, Reiffenstuel offers the power of absolving from reserved sins, or, of dispensing, or any power of a similar nature.

There is no doubt that there is a difference between privileges contrary to the law, and privileges beyond the law. But whether there is always a clearly defined root-difference between these two classes of privilege is another question. Reiffenstuel himself [16] calls a privilege beyond the law a privilege, but he adds *potius dicitur beneficium principis.*

Schmalzgrueber scarcely goes beyond Reiffenstuel's definition of a privilege beyond the law.[17] Like Reiffenstuel he adds: *privilegium praeter ius non est ita stricte privilegium sed potius dicitur beneficium principis, seu gratia ab isto concessa.*

Suarez[18] taking up the idea of *beneficium principis*

---

14 Motry, *o.c.*, p. 39.
15 Reiffenstuel, *o.c.*, lib. V, tit. XXXIII, n. 7.
16 Reiffenstuel, *o.c.*, lib. V, tit. XXXIII, n. 8.
17 Schmalzgrueber, *o.c.*, lib. V, tit. XXXIII, n. 57-58.
18 Suarez, *o.c.*, lib. VIII, cap. I, n. 5.

claims that all privileges can be reduced to this concept. Therefore, merely because of the predominance of this element in privileges beyond the law, it would be improper to deny the name privilege to such privileges as powers of absolving, dispensing, etc.

Wernz,[19] who censures Hinschius' absolute denial of *privilegia praeter ius*, says *multae facultates**** merito dicuntur privilegia quia constituunt leges privatas concedentes specialem favorem, licet minus strictum.*

The authors just enumerated are indicative of the canonical doctrine taught before the Code.[20] Hence, if Suarez be for the moment eliminated, it will be evident that Reiffenstuel and Schmalzgrueber teach that a privilege beyond the law is only improperly called a privilege. Wernz will not grant so much, but he does admit that such a privilege is *minus strictum.* Can it be that privileges beyond the law formed a class of privileges distinct in themselves, a division which could be accommodated to privileges only in a broad sense?

Suarez is logical in maintaining that all privileges are in some way *beneficia principis.*[21] He thinks that the whole discussion may be merely concerning a name. This is true if the origin alone of privileges be the point of discussion. Beyond this Suarez's contention can hardly be admitted. The use of the two classes of privilege have little in common. Besides this, the question of interpretation brings the difference into bold relief. Privileges contrary to the law are to be strictly interpreted,[22] while privileges beyond the law are to be interpreted broadly. Such wide divergence can scarcely be called *questio de nomine.*

A consideration of the opinions set down seems to

---

19 Wernz, *o.c.*, v. I, n. 158, ft. 15.

20 The same doctrine is held today by De Meester, *o.c.*, n. 305.

21 Suarez, *o.c.*, l.c.

22 Reiffenstuel, *o.c.*, lib. V, tit. XXXIII, n. 9; Schmalzgrueber, *o.c.*, lib. V, tit. XXXIII, n. 58.

reveal that before the Code privileges beyond the law held a somewhat indefinite position. Midway between a privilege contrary to the law and *beneficium principis* would probably be the proper place for a privilege beyond the law. Yet even this juxtaposition can hardly be urged too strongly for an examination of privileges beyond the law shows that they tend to one or the other of the extremes, either they will lean toward a privilege contrary to the law, or they will suggest *beneficium principis.*

In order to observe the tendency towards privileges contrary to the law, it is necessary to consider the universal and exclusive binding-force of the law itself. In the laws which concede powers of absolving, or dispensing, the beneficiaries are determined. Should this power be granted to one not comprehended in the law, *radicaliter* the concession is in some way contrary to the law, and not merely beyond it. But if consideration be restricted to the immediate characteristic of this concession of power, Reiffenstuel's definition of a privilege beyond the law can be accepted because the new beneficiary is not one of those to whom the law itself concedes the power of absolving, or dispensing.[28]

On the other hand, a privilege beyond the law may tend toward the concept of a pure *beneficium principis.* This is revealed in the nature of such concessions as faculties to bestow special blessings.

For practical purposes, considering the almost unanimous grouping of powers of absolving, dispensing, and the like under the head of privileges beyond the law, it is best to retain the traditional classification, and con-

---

28 Reiffenstuel, *o.c.*, lib. V, tit. XXXIII, n. 7.

tinue to refer to such concessions as privileges beyond the law.

The new Code does not settle the discussion concerning privileges beyond the law. But, while the use of the word *accensentur* (accenseo) to reckon in addition, to add to,[24] does not definitely place privileges beyond the law in the category of privileges properly so-called, it does show that the mind of the legislator leans toward this classification. And more: the use of the term *praeter ius* would seem to approve this class of privileges. Thus from authentic usage the continued and legitimate use of the classification can be maintained.

With the completion of the foregoing discussion, the question arises what faculties are to be numbered among the privileges beyond the law. A faculty can be actual, or habitual according to the duration of the power conceded. Canon 66, § 1 limits the terminology of privilege beyond the law to habitual faculties. Which faculties are to be considered in this light are enumerated, viz., faculties conceded in perpetuity, or for a definite time, or, finally, for a certain number of cases. Faculties conceded in perpetuity can hardly be understood properly of personal faculties. While it is true that a personal faculty may be said to be perpetual in the sense that it may last as long as the grantee lives, yet such perpetuity is only relative. A faculty conceded for a definite limit of time, or for a certain number of cases may be either personal or real, *i. e.,* attached to the position of the Ordinary. The rescript will usually settle doubts. But if the rescript should not be explicit, the second paragraph of canon 66 will settle the matter.

---

24 John White, *Latin-English Dictionary,* v. accenseo, (New York, no date).

**Canon 66, § 2. Nisi in earum concessione electa fuerit industria personae aut aliud expresse cautum sit, facultates habituales, Episcopo aliisve de quibus in can. 198, § 1 ab Apostolica Sede concessae, non evanescunt, resoluto iure Ordinarii cui concessae sunt, etiamsi ipse eas exsequi coeperit, sed transeunt ad Ordinarios qui ipsi in regimine succedunt; item concessae Episcopo competunt quoque Vicario Generali.**

When Putzer published his commentary on Apostolic Faculties[25] such grants were considered practically in the light of personal privileges. Unless special mention of communication, or sub-delegation were made, the faculties had to be exercised personally. The further conclusion was that such faculties could not pass to successors in office. There was indeed a restricted communication allowed but it concerned the missionaries who labored in places where the exercise of the Catholic religion was forbidden. This concession read: *Communicandi has facultates in totum vel in partem, prout opus esse secundum eius conscientiam indicaverit, sacerdotibus idoneis in conversione animarum laborantibus, in locis tantum ubi prohibetur exercitium catholicae religionis.*[26] The Sacred Penitentiary, answering a request that an interpretation be given concerning a particular case in France, and in Europe generally, replied that the Bishop should consult the Congregation of the Inquisition.

In 1889 the Holy Office was asked to settle a question in regard to habitual delegation of faculties of dispensing from matrimonial impediments *in periculo mortis.* The Holy Office would not decide the matter itself, but referred the request to the Pope. The Holy Father received the request kindly and allowed habitual delegation

---

25 Konings-Putzer, *o.c.*, n. 28-29.
26 Coll. n. 1695.

to be made to parish priests only (not to all approved confessors), provided there would not be sufficient time to approach the Ordinary, and at the same time a danger existed in delay.[27]

On November 24, 1897, the Holy Office, considering the circumstances of the times, determined to petition the Pope to declare that habitual matrimonial faculties conceded to Ordinaries[28] did not cease with their death, or loss of office, but instead passed to their successors in office. Pope Leo XIII acceded to the petition; *atque ita perpetuis futuris temporibus servandam mandavit, contrariis non obstantibus quibuscumque.*[29] Immediately the question arose concerning faculties conceded to Bishops anterior to this decree. Were they to be considered as attached to the office of the grantee rather than to his person? The Holy Office decided that the extension of Pope Leo XIII was to include the faculties granted before November 24, 1897,[30] *facto verbo cum Sanctissimo.*

The Holy Office made a further concession on December 14, 1898. To the question: *An possit Episcopus diocesanus subdelegare, absque speciali concessione, suis Vicariis Generalibus aut aliis ecclesiasticis viris modo generali, vel saltem pro casu particulari, facultates ab Apostolica Sede sibi ad tempus delegatas,* the Holy Office replied *Affirmative, dummodo id in facultatibus non prohibeatur, neque subdelegandi ius pro aliquibus tantum coarctetur; in hoc enim casu servanda erit forma adamussim Rescripti.*[31]

27 Coll. n. 1698.

28 The word "Ordinary" was used according to the decree of February 20, 1888, (Coll. n. 1685). *Appellatione Ordinarii venire Episcopos, Administratores seu Vicarios Apostolicos, Praelatos seu Praefectos habentes iurisdictionem cum territorio separato, eorumque officiales seu Vicarios in spiritualibus generales, et sede vacante Vicarium Capitularem et legitimum Administratorem.*

29 Coll. n. 1985.

30 Coll. ft. to n. 1985, June 23, 1898; Coll. n. 2094, September 5, 1900.

31 Coll. n. 2029.

The continuation of faculties conceded to Ordinaries of a place, but limited to a definite time was provided for in the decision of the Holy Office under the date of May 3, 1899.[32] Towards the end of the same year, December 20, 1899, an extension was asked for the faculties of all superiors. The Pope, thru the Holy Office, granted the extension *ad Superiores generales Ordinum religiosorum.*[33]

The legislation of the new Code incorporates the ruling of the Holy Office of November 24, 1897. The general principle to be followed, then, is that habitual faculties do not cease with their grantee's loss of power. The Code refers to the list of those whose faculties enjoy this continuance. Canon 198, §1 states who are the Ordinaries in law. Besides the Roman Pontiff, such Ordinaries are residential Bishops, Abbots and Prelates *nullius,* together with Vicar Generals, Administrators, Vicars and Prefects Apostolic.[34] All these are *Ordinarii locorum.* In addition to these Ordinaries are to be considered the major Superiors of exempt clerical religious. Canon 488, n. 8 specifies who are major superiors. They are: Abbot Primates, Abbot Superior of a monastic congregation, Abbot of a monastery *sui iuris* even if it belongs to a monastic congregation, Supreme Moderator of a religion, Provincial Superior, their Vicars and, lastly, those who have provincial power *ad instar.*

The *resoluto iure Ordinarii* may occur in several ways. Death, removal, renunciation of office, all may dissolve the connection between an Ordinary and his office. Suspension, however, does not dissolve this link, but merely holds it in abeyance until the penalty is removed.

---

32 Coll. n. 2045.

33 Coll. n. 2074.

34 To these Ordinaries must now be added the Vicar Delegates, instituted by Pope Benedict XV, AAS. v. XII, p. 120.

Similarly exile, and physical incapacity do not cause loss of jurisdictional power.[35]

The continuity of faculties is not broken even if the Ordinary began to exercise his faculties before he lost his office.

With the loss of the Ordinary's power, faculties pass to his successor in office. The constitution of a diocese, vicariate, or prefecture will determine the Ordinary's successor. In places where a cathedral chapter is erected, the immediate successor of the Ordinary will be the same cathedral chapter.[36] The Canons of the cathedral chapter enjoy succession until they have elected a Vicar Capitular. This must be done within eight days *ab accepta notitia vacationis.*[37] Where no cathedral chapter exists, the power of the Ordinary passes to the body of diocesan consultors.[38] They, too, enjoy succession until they have elected an Administrator. This also must be done within eight days *ab accepta notitia vacationis.* In vicariates and prefectures, provided no Co-adjutor with right of succession is named, the successor of the Vicar, or Prefect will be the pro-Vicar, or pro-Prefect.[39] These latter officials have no ordinary power as long as the Vicar, or Prefect retains his office. Accordingly, the pro-Vicar, and the pro-Prefect are not the same as the Vicar Delegate conceded by Pope Benedict XV.[40]

In an abbey, or a prelacy *nullius* succession devolves upon the religious chapter, should the benefice pertain to the religious. The constitutions of the religious, however, may legally dispose otherwise. If the prelacy belongs to seculars, the canonical chapter or its equivalent succeeds. Both the religious, and the canonical chapters

35 Can. 429.
36 Can. 431, § 1; can. 435, § 2.
37 Can. 432, § 1.
38 Can. 427.
39 Can. 309, § 2.
40 Winslow, *Prefects and Vicars Apostolic,* (New York, 1924) p. 65-74.

must elect a Vicar Capitular within eight days. During the interim, the chapter enjoys the jurisdiction of the Ordinary.[41]

These are the ordinary methods of succession. In addition to these the Code provides for two unusual contingencies. Canon 431, §2 concedes the power of Vicar Capitular to the Archbishop, or Bishop who may have been named by the Holy See, as Administrator of a vacant diocese. Canon 309, §4 supposes the non-existence of a pro-Vicar, or a pro-Prefect. In this case the senior priest of the vicariate, or prefecture succeeds in office. This seniority is determined both by actual residence in the territory, and from the time when the proper letters were first exhibited. Should two or more priests enjoy the same seniority, the successor of the Ordinary will be selected according to seniority of ordination.

Canon 66, § 2 makes two exceptions to the general principle concerning the continuation of faculties. First, the rescript containing the habitual faculties may stipulate that the concession lapses with the death, removal, etc., of the grantee. Or, secondly, habitual faculties may be conceded to an Ordinary because of some special merit, or uncommon qualifications which the grantee possesses. Such concessions are called *industria personae.*[42]

The first exception to the general principle requires no comment. The rescript must be examined for possible clauses restricting the continuation of the faculties. But the second exception to the general principle entails some explanation. How is the peculiar nature of the faculties granted *industria personae* to be recognized?

It has just been observed that faculties granted *industria personae* are conceded to an individual Ordinary for reasons of his unusual merit in some special field of activity. What would influence the grantor to concede

---

41 Can. 327, § 1.
42 Blat, *o.c.*, v. I, n. 134.

such peculiar faculties will vary in different circumstances. Detailed and exact knowledge will offer a reason in one case, uncommon circumspection in another. In a word, personal merit of a high and unusual caliber will supply a reason.

What must be noticed in faculties of this kind is that the personal fitness of the grantee is emphasized.

With these thoughts in mind it is not difficult to see why faculties conceded *industria personae* do not pass to a successor in office. With the grantee's loss of power, the faculties cease. The reason of this cessation is to be found in the restricted will of the legislator rather than in the successor's possible deficiency in regard to unusual merits. If, in point of fact, a successor should possess the same, or even greater qualities, the faculties would cease even in this case because of the personal element of the predecessor's faculties.

Faculties granted *industria personae* will contain expressions which will leave no doubt, ordinarily speaking, of their nature. Such expressions as *propter profundam scientiam qua polles in re,* or *committimus prudentiae tuae eximiae* leave little doubt of the personal nature of the faculties. But the mere reference to *prudentia* does not imply the same thing as prudence is expected in every Superior. Neither would the mere mention of the Bishop's name always signify that his faculties were granted *industria personae.*[43]

Since the personal element is a restriction placed on the use and continuation of habitual faculties, proof must be adduced to demonstrate this restriction. The presumption is in favor of the continuation of faculties, *resoluto iure Ordinarii.*[44]

The Code makes no provision for the continuation of faculties granted to Superiors of non-exempt religious.

---

43 Maroto, *o.c.*, v. I, n. 294.

44 Maroto, *o.c.*, l.c., Ayrinhac, *o.c.*, n. 171.

Maroto[45] considers these faculties to continue if they were granted to the Superiors without mentioning their name. In this case the faculties would be real, not personal. But if the name of the Superior were mentioned together with his dignity, the faculties would be personal and cease with the office of Superior. Maroto hesitates to urge the last provision in an unqualified statement. Perhaps, he says, even then the faculties may appear to be real, and not personal faculties. Cocchi does not commit himself but cites Maroto's opinion. However, he adds that not a few authors maintain the dignity overshadows the name of the Superior and, hence, the faculties can be considered as real and as passing to successors in office.[46]

In the absence of positive legislation on this point, recurrence is to be made to similar legislation.[47] Therefore, it may be assumed that the personal element of faculties granted to Superiors of non-exempt religious must be proved. Otherwise, the faculties may be considered as real, and, hence, as passing to successors in office, according to the provision of canon 66, § 2. The mere mention of the Superior's name can hardly be sufficient evidence of a faculty granted *industria personae*. Something more specific, as expected for Ordinaries, would be required.

The faculties conceded to a Bishop are likewise to be understood of the Vicar General. The origin of the Vicar General is not undisputed. Wernz seeks his origin in the *officialis principalis*,[48] while Fournier sees his first appearance in the procurator general.[49] Which-

---

45 Maroto, *o.c.*, l.c.
46 Cocchi, *o.c.*, v. I, n. 123.
47 Can. 20.
48 Wernz-Vidal, *De Personis*, (Romae, 1923) n. 634.
49 Fournier, *Les Origines du Vicaire General*, (Paris, 1922) p. 73.

ever origin may finally be accepted, it is certain that the office developed greatly during the years 1234-1298.[50]

The present discipline concerning the Vicar General is found in canons 366-371. Formerly, a residential Bishop, or Abbot, or Prelate *nullius* were the only ones who could nominate a Vicar General. But Pope Benendict XV granted a similar right to Vicars and Prefects Apostolic. The new officials were to be called Vicar Delegates, and were to have practically the same power as Vicar Generals.[51]

Briefly, the Vicar General is competent, by ordinary power, in everything that pertains to the jurisdiction of his Bishop unless the Code demand a special mandate, or the Bishop himself reserve some power.[52] Unless the contrary is evident, a Vicar General can execute Apostolic rescripts committed to his diocese.[53] Ordinarily, the Vicar General should not be nominated a judge.[54] A paucity of trials, or the small size of the diocese may excuse from this recommendation of the Code.

In what faculties conceded to a Bishop, are the Vicar Generals similarly competent? Undoubtedly all the habitual faculties which the Bishop enjoys, unless the rescript determine otherwise, or the faculties be conceded to the Bishop *industria personae.* Theoretically the two exceptions may be considered separately, but practically they amount to the same thing. The rescript will reveal whether or not the personal characteristics and qualities of the Bishop are responsible for the faculties. Just as for non-continuation, so also for exclusive use this *industria personae* must be proved. The presumption is that the faculties are conceded to the Ordi-

50 Wernz-Vidal, *o.c.,* l.c.
51 Wernz-Vidal, *o.c.,* n. 636.
52 Can. 368, § 1.
53 Can. 368, § 2.
54 Can. 1573, § 1.

nary as such without any special emphasis on the Bishop's personal qualifications.

Can a Bishop restrict the faculties to his own personal execution? Obviously if the faculties were granted to him *industria personae,* or if the rescript plainly so state, he must do so. In regard to the other habitual faculties, the Bishop is powerless to restrict the Vicar General in the use of the faculties. The argument from the restriction which a Bishop may lawfully put upon his Vicar General,[55] will not hold in the case of faculties. The former is ordinary jurisdiction [56] and the Bishop is empowered to limit it: the latter is a privilege granted by the Holy See in which the Bishop is granted no limiting powers. The Code says expressly without limitation, *item concessae (facultates habituales) competunt quoque Vicario Generali.*

A Vicar General, however, who is the *alter ego* of the Bishop of the diocese, should use the faculties according to the legitimate wishes of the Bishop. But if the Vicar General does not act in this way, his acts are valid, no matter how many restrictions the Bishop of his own accord may place on the use of the faculties.

**Canon 66, § 3. Concessa facultas secumfert alias quoque potestates quae ad illius usum sunt necessariae; quare in facultate dispensandi includitur etiam potestas absolvendi a poenis ecclesiasticis, si quae obstent, sed ad effectum dumtaxat dispensationis consequendae.**

A brief reference to the efficient cause of a privilege is necessary. It is the will of the legislator, or Superior which attributes power, or efficacy to a privilege. In most instances a Superior will couch his concession in explicit terms so that the extent of the power granted can easily be understood. In the case of habitual facul-

55 Can. 368, § 1.
56 Chelodi, *o.c.*, n. 200.

ties, the power connected with the exercise of a faculty is extended to include other powers which may be accessory but necessary to the use of the faculty.

The footnotes in the Code to canon 66, § 3 refer to Rules 35, 42, 53, and 80 in Sexto Bonifacii VIII. The gist of all four rules is contained in the first part of canon 66, § 3. Even before the Pontificate of Boniface VIII, Pope Alexander III several times conceded all necessary powers to fulfill a delegation in judicial cases.[57] There never was any real denial of the principle: *Cui licet quod est plus, licet utique quod est minus.*[58] The concession of power over interfering persons, or circumstances sometimes was so explicit that, at first sight, no legitimate proportion seems to exist between judge and accused. Witness the power which Alexander III concedes in a letter to the Bishop of Chartres. By this letter a delegated judge, because of the august personage he represents, enjoys the power of compelling with penalties even a Bishop, or a higher dignitary.[59] Calm judgment, however must guide a judge in these matters. Pope Alexander III emphasized this point in the same letter to the Bishop of Chartres: *iudex secundum negotii qualitatem temperate procedens.*

Blat says[60] that the implied faculties of canon 66, § 3 are conceded according to the nature of the faculty which is expressly granted. This is true, but the use of the word "object" (*obiectum*) rather than "nature" (*natura*) would obviate difficulties. "*Natura*" considers the juridical and philosophical notions which enter into the composition of a faculty. In this sense there is no difference between faculties, as, for instance, be-

---

57 C. 1, 5, 11, X, *de officio et potestate iudicis delegati,* I, 29.

58 R.J. 53 in VI. The other rules referred to in the footnote to canon 66, 3, are: Regula 35, *Plus semper in se continet quod est minus;* Regula 42, *Accessorium naturam sequi congruit principalis;* Regula 80, *In toto partem non est dubium contineri.*

59 C. 11, X, *de officio et potestate iudicis delegati,* I, 29.

60 Blat, *o.c.,* v. I, n. 134.

tween judicial and administrative faculties. "*Obiectum,*" however, considers the external qualities of a faculty. Thus faculties may be judicial, administrative, *pro foro interno, pro foro externo*, etc.

The use of implied powers must be limited to those that are necessary for the valid and licit use of the faculty itself. To go beyond this would be to extend one's jurisdiction contrary to the will of the Superior who granted the faculty. Since such excesses are not allowed, the unauthorized acts would be invalid.[61]

Canonical equity must also be taken into consideration in the use of implied powers. Therefore, reasonable exceptions according to law must be admitted.[62]

The Code itself illustrates the concession of accessory but necessary faculties in the execution of a dispensation. The implication is that absolution from censure is considered to be a minor element in relation to the use of the faculty itself. Strictly speaking, absolution from censure, and fruition of a dispensation are not in the same category. But because of the efficacious will of the legislator, everything necessary for the valid and licit use of a faculty is conceded. Yet it must be borne in mind, as the Code specifically declares, the absolution from penalties can be given only in direct relation to the execution of the faculty.

In the case of matrimonial faculties, the Sacred Congregation of the Propaganda gave a decision on September 26, 1821.[63] The question concerned the possibly necessary absolution from the censure of major excommunication. The doubt was proposed concerning both the internal and the external forum. The Congregation decided that an absolution *ad cautelam* must be given in the internal forum, but that a new faculty for the exter-

61 C. 11, *de rescriptis,* I, 3 in VI.
62 C. 13, 15, X, *de officio et potestate iudicis,* I, 29.
63 Coll. n. 769.

nal forum would be necessary. The latter stipulation may seem to be an undue restriction, but such is not really the case. It is merely an exemplification of the principle that public penalties should cease in some public way so that a public scandal may be properly repaired. On July 2, 1891,[64] the Sacred Penitentiary praised an Ordinary who followed the practice of the Sacred Penitentiary, and the Apostolic Datary in prefixing an absolution from censures *ad cautelam*.

The importance of a previous absolution from censure was founded upon the inability which such a penalty caused. Until 1918, heretics, schismatics, false and recalled procurators, excommunicated persons *excommunicatione maiore* were excluded from receiving favors.[65] Pius X changed the law considerably, restricting inability to those who were excommunicated by name, or who were suspended *a divinis* by the Holy See.[66] The Code introduced another change[67] in the law. The present discipline allows everyone, even censured persons, to enjoy favors unless the censure (excommunication, interdict, suspension) be inflicted by a condemnatory or declaratory sentence.[68]

The necessity, then, of previous absolution from censure is considerably diminished at the present time. All undispensed vindictive penalties will not invalidate favors, nor unabsolved censures where no sentence has intervened. It is evident that the implied faculties conceded in canon 66, § 3 are not as essential to the dispensation as formerly.[69]

---

64 Coll. n. 1759.
65 Wernz, *o.c.*, v. I, n. 151.
66 Ordo servandus in S. Congregationibus, Tribunalibus, Officiis Romanae Curiae, 29 Sept., 1908, Pars II, Normae peculiares, cap. III, n. 6, A.A.S., v. I, p. 64.
67 Can. 36, § 2.
68 Can. 2265, § 2; 2275, § 3; 2283.
69 Vermeersch-Creusen, *o.c.*, v. I, n. 133.

Universitas Catholica Americae

Washingtonii, D. C.

Facultas Iuris Canonici

1925-1926

No. 35

DEUS LUX MEA

---

# THESES

QUAS

AD DOCTORATUS GRADUM

IN

# IURE CANONICO

**Apud Universitatem Catholicam Americae**

CONSEQUENDUM

PUBLICE PROPUGNABIT

EDUARDUS G. ROELKER, S. T. D., J. C. L.,

SACERDOS ARCHIDIOECESIS CINCINNATENSIS.

---

HORA IX-XI, A. M. DIE XXIX MAII A. D. MCMXXVI.

---

I. De Ecclesia ut Societate.

II. De Elemento Aristocratico in Ecclesia.

III. De Regio Placet.

IV. De Status Separatione ab Ecclesia.

V. De Concordatis.

VI. De Sexto Bonifacii VIII.

| | | |
|---|---|---|
| VII. | Canones 12-14. | De Subiecto Legis Ecclesiasticae. |
| VIII. | Canones 17-20. | De Interpretatione Legum. |
| IX. | Canon 105. | De Validitate actus Superioris absque Consensu vel Consilio aliquarum Personarum. |
| X. | Canon 106. | De Iure Praecedentiae. |
| XI. | Canones 248, 255. | De S. C. Consistoriali, et de S. C. pro Negotiis ecclesiasticis extraordinariis. |
| XII. | Canones 329-332. | De Nominatione et Dotibus Episcopi. |
| XIII. | Canones 339, 466. | De Applicatione Missae pro Populo. |
| XIV. | Canones 340-342. | De Relatione super Statu Diocesis, et de Visitatione *ad limina*. |
| XV. | Canones 350-355. | De Coadiutoribus et Auxiliaribus Episcoporum. |
| XVI. | Canones 464-5, 467-470. | De praecipuis Obligationibus Parochorum. |

| | | |
|---|---|---|
| XVII. | Canones 487-491. | De Religiosis in genere. |
| XVIII. | Canones 520-521. | De Confessario ordinario, speciali, et extraordinario. |
| XIX. | Canones 542-552. | De Requisitis ut quis in novitiatum admittatur. |
| XX. | Canones 572-573. | De Requisitis ad validam Professionem religiosam. |
| XXI. | Canones 574, 577-578. | De Votis temporariis ante Professionem perpetuam. |
| XXII. | Canones 579-583. | De Voto Paupertatis quoad Professionem simplicem et solemnem. |
| XXIII. | Canones 845-852. | De Ministro Sacrae Communionis. |
| XXIV. | Canones 901-907. | De Subiecto Sacramenti Poenitentiae. |
| XXV. | Canones 973-982. | De Requisitis in Subiecto Sacrae Ordinationis. |
| XXVI. | Canones 1002-1005. | De Ritibus et Caeremoniis sacrae Ordinationis. |
| XXVII. | Canones 1074-1075. | De Impedimentis Raptus et Criminis. |
| XXVIII. | Canones 1128-1132. | De Separatione Tori, Mensae, et Habitationis. |

| | | |
|---|---|---|
| XXIX. | Canones 1197-1202. | De Altaribus. |
| XXX. | Canones 1613-1614. | De Causis a Iudice non suscipiendis et de Iudice suspecto. |
| XXXI. | Canones 1636-1639. | De Loco et Tempore Iudicii. |
| XXXII. | Canones 1789-1791. | De Testimoniorum Fide. |
| XXXIII. | Canones 1812-1818. | De Natura et Fide Instrumentorum. |
| XXXIV. | Canones 1960-1965. | De Foro competenti in Causis Matrimonialibus. |
| XXXV. | Canones 1986-1989. | De Appellationibus in Causis Matrimonialibus. |
| XXXVI. | Canones 2186-2194. | De Modo procedendi in Suspensione ex informata Conscientia infligenda. |
| XXXVII. | Canones 2217-2219. | De Poenarum Speciebus, Interpretatione atque Applicatione. |
| XXXVIII. | Canones 2286-2290. | De Poenis vindicativis in genere. |
| XXXIX. | Canones 2306-2313. | De Remediis poenalibus et de Poenitentiis. |

## ROMAN LAW

XL. Sources and Division of *Codex Iuris Civilis.*
XLI. Enslavement.
XLII. Release from Slavery.
XLIII. Position, Duties and Rights of *Colonus.*
XLIV. *Non-Cives.*
XLV. Modification of Personality.
XLVI. Extinction of Personality.
XLVII. Origin of Citizenship.
XLVIII. Concept, Form and Conditions of Matrimony.
XLIX. Tutelage in Roman Law.
L. Possession.

## INTERNATIONAL LAW.

LI. Meaning of International Law.
LII. Sources of International Law.
LIII. General Rights of States.
LIV. Self-preservation and Intervention.
LV. Immunity.
LVI. Consuls.
LVII. Extradition.
LVIII. Piracy.
LIX. Drago Doctrine.
LX. Monroe Doctrine.

* * * * * *

VIDIT FACULTAS:
PHILIPPUS BERNADINI, S. T. D., J. U. D., Decanus.
H. LUDOVICUS MOTRY, S. T. D., J. C. D., p. t. a Secretis.

VIDIT RECTOR UNIVERSITATIS:
†THOMAS J. SHAHAN, S. T. D., J. U. L.

## VITA.

Edward G. Roelker was born in Cincinnati, Ohio, August 16, 1897. After attending the parochial school of Saint Mary he entered Saint Francis Xavier High School and College in Cincinnati. In 1918 he entered Mount Saint Mary of the West Seminary, and a year later entered the North American College, Rome, Italy. On May 26, 1923, he was ordained to the Holy Priesthood and in June, 1924, was awarded the Degree of Doctor of Theology.

Father Roelker entered the Catholic University of America in September, 1924, to pursue a post-graduate course in Canon Law. Father Roelker extends his sincerest thanks to the professors who have assisted him with their kind suggestions. The writer also wishes to thank the assistant librarian for the freedom accorded him in consulting the valuable works of the University Library.

www.ingramcontent.com/pod-product-compliance
Lightning Source LLC
LaVergne TN
LVHW050230080826
844660LV00012B/504

* 9 7 8 0 8 1 3 2 2 2 2 5 7 *